Starting A Successful Airbnb Business for Beginners

How to Start Investing in Short Term Rentals, Profit from Your First Property, and Create a Model for Extra Monthly Income Now

Davis J Miller

for Beast, the best dog in the world!

2006-2021

Do Something Today Your Future Self Will
Thank You For

Table of Contents

From The Author

If you picked up this book, it means you have been thinking about becoming an Airbnb host. Congratulations!

You have taken the first step towards embarking on this exciting new journey. I'm here to share, with you, the secrets to setting up your own successful Airbnb business.

I remember when I first started. It all happened after I stayed at my first Airbnb. With my love for business and travel, plus an interest in real estate investing, I fell in love with their business model, instantly. However, it took me a while to start. There were so many questions I had, not to mention, so many fears. I took to the internet and invested a considerable amount of time into researching how Airbnb works and how it would align with my real estate investing goals.

What happened then? I did some more research. And then some more research...and then some more. Finally, the day came when I realized **I was the one holding myself back!**

The day I realized this, was the day I decided to take the plunge. Once I overcame the "procrastination bug", started my own Airbnb, and experienced the feeling of getting my first booking, I decided I would not let procrastination get the best of me anymore. This attitude allowed me to start and keep going, no matter how hard I thought it would be. I felt unstoppable! I began to apply my years of business experience to my research and was able to use this information to set up my first property and become an Airbnb Superhost myself. I realized a whole new world of opportunities are on the other side of procrastination and it became my passion to help others change their lives, and get out of their own way, too.

It's my pleasure to share my own insights with you and help you break free of procrastination in order to create your own success.

Allow Me to Be Your Guide

You've done your research – maybe *too* much research (like me) – and you still haven't started yet.

Is it because you are thinking the market is oversaturated and it's too late to get into the Airbnb game? *It's not!*

Are you concerned you don't have enough business savvy to make your Airbnb business a success? *You do!*

Or, have you become overwhelmed by all the "authorities" out there who want to help you - the "YouTubers" selling thousand-dollar courses or the hundreds of books claiming they have all the answers without being based on actual experience?

While you may be attracted to the idea of the financial independence that can come from starting this business, I'm betting you still worry about how you can possibly make it happen.

This is where I come in. I can help by sharing with you, the secrets to setting up your new venture. In fact, my goal for this book is to give you the know-how and confidence you need to start a successful Airbnb business.

But first, there is something I need from you. Everyone has it in them to do this business and a lot of people have the potential, but they never take ACTION. That is all I ask from you – is to take action, NOW! Meaning, start to implement what you learn ASAP.

This book is meant to set you up for success. It is not meant to be read through once, only to be put away on a shelf after you're finished. Use this book as your guide, to reference at any point in your journey.

To help you on your journey, you will find at the end of each chapter, ***Action Items to DO NOW!*** These are steps you can take, immediately, after reading each chapter to keep you from procrastinating and FINALLY be on your way to starting your own Airbnb business.

Let's do this!

Davis J. Miller

Are You Ready for a Change?

I understand what it's like to be trapped in a numbing, unrewarding 9-to-5 job and wanting to find a way to achieve financial freedom.

Waking up to an insistent alarm early in the morning, struggling to get showered and dressed, grabbing a quick bite to eat, and then rushing out the door in time to make it to work.

Once you're at work you spend a long, boring, and stressful day making money for other people. Then, you head home in the evening to recharge as best you can before going through the same routine the next day... and the next...

You start to think you live for the weekend. But what's the weekend? As soon as it arrives, it's Monday again! You're back to thinking "Friday can't come fast enough, can it?". You're in a never-ending cycle you can't get out of. After all, you need the job to survive.

Does this sound like your life?

You are not alone, of course. So many people spend their lives simply worrying about paying the bills and trying to save some money without ever finding joy in what they're doing.

What if I told you there's a way you can break loose from the daily grind, make more money than ever before, AND have the freedom that comes with being your own boss?

Let's face it, as long as you are working for someone else, whether it's a huge corporation or a small business, you aren't going to reap the rewards of your hard work.

Whatever you get paid and whatever benefits you receive, it's the owners who get to keep the big profits.

However, if you start your own Airbnb business, you get to be the boss who makes the money. Isn't that an attractive prospect?

The Airbnb model has provided millions of hosts all around the world with either a reliable stream of side income or enough to create a full-time job that puts them in the driver's seat.

You could start paying off your mortgage, saving money for your children's education or setting up a retirement fund for yourself.

Maybe you will have the chance to travel more? Or buy a new car? Whatever you choose to do with your extra income, it's yours! Not your employer's.

What You'll Learn in this Book

This book will take you through the steps you need to start your own Airbnb and fill your calendar with reservations.

Is owning an Airbnb a side-hustle or a full-time job? Do you want to be a hands-on host, or turn your property into a source of passive income? First, we will define your goals so you know the direction you will be headed.

Then, we'll move on to how the Airbnb business model works and what you need to do to get started on your own.

Finding the ideal property to start your Airbnb business can be a challenge. However, I will share my experience to help you find a great place in the right location and close on your property.

Once you have your property, we will talk about how to set up the space to make it a warm, welcoming, and desirable destination for your guests.

Next, I'll walk you through every step of the mechanics of listing your property on Airbnb, helping you avoid any potential pitfalls.

After that, we'll run through the essentials of what it takes to be a great host who will consistently rack up the 5-star reviews you need to succeed.

Closer to the end, I'll provide some guidance on how to grow and scale your Airbnb business to achieve even greater success down the road.

Finally...

You know what your current reality is. Now, imagine...

Using your creativity and skills to turn an empty house into a beautiful, welcoming getaway for your guests.

Developing an income stream that can either supplement your current income or replace it.

Enjoying increased financial independence as your Airbnb business grows and expands.

Let's get started making this possibility your new reality!

Action Item to DO NOW!

1. Make a commitment to yourself you will stop procrastinating and start *now*!

CHAPTER ONE

Why Are You Choosing This Venture?

S tarting your own short-term rental business is an attractive prospect. Before plunging in, you need to define WHY you want to do it – your reason and motivation for wanting to operate an Airbnb business.

Not only do you have to determine whether this is a good move for you financially or personally, you also need to know your passion behind it. This is a beneficial exercise for any entrepreneur to help remind them of the purpose for choosing this venture. It helps keep your eye on the goals you set (more to come on this) as you are going through the ups and downs of your journey.

Take some time to jot down *why* you are choosing to invest in an Airbnb property. Then, post it somewhere you will see it, often. For example, take a photo of it and make it the home screen photo on your phone.

When determining your "why" think about the Airbnb business you want to have and *why* you want it – what inspires you to do this?

Start by asking yourself: "why do you want to have an Airbnb business?".

Instead of simply wanting to do this because you have an extra room or two in your home or a cottage or vacation home sitting empty between visits, your "why" should be the driving force behind your decision to choose this path.

Are you looking for an additional revenue stream to supplement or replace your current income?

Do you want to take your family on more vacations?

Maybe you really want to create a completely self-sufficient career and lifestyle?

All of these are reasons why someone could want to start an Airbnb business.

What is yours?

Why Airbnb Started

Airbnb got its start in San Francisco in 2007. Roommates Joe Gebbia and Brian Chesky noticed all the hotel rooms were sold out ahead of an industrial design conference, and they saw an opportunity to cover their rent (their "why", perhaps?).

They bought some air mattresses and set up a rudimentary website advertising accommodations on their living room floor with breakfast in the morning, for $80 a night. Three people signed up and they had their first "Air-Bed-N-Breakfast". They also acted as guides for their guests, showing them San Francisco as the inhabitants knew it (not just as tourists) and they loved the experience as much as their guests.

They brought Nathan Blecharczyk on board in January 2008 to set up a more robust website. One of their most important innovations was routing all payments through the site, removing any awkwardness from in-person monetary transactions.

After an early flop at South by Southwest (SXSW), their first success was booking accommodations for the Democratic convention in Denver in 2008, for which they created custom Obama and McCain-themed cereal boxes to advertise their website and raise money to keep the company afloat. Soon after, they started to attract the attention of investors who gave them start-up capital.

Since then, of course, Airbnb has become a giant of the accommodation business and is still growing today.

What is Airbnb Now?

Airbnb is an internet platform that brings together hosts and travelers. It has revolutionized the short-term rental (STR) industry making it easier for anyone to get into this space. Hosts have the ability to rent out a single room in a city apartment all the way up to operating dozens of separate properties across several states or countries.

Since this new business model began, it has become a huge success with 2.9 million active hosts in 2022, in countries around the globe. An average of 14,000 new hosts sign up each month on the platform.

The average host in the United States earns about $9,000 annually and renting out a full apartment as an Airbnb property can net you more than $31,000 a year in popular destinations such as Miami and San Diego.

You can see how building a portfolio of multiple properties can soon become a full-time career with substantial returns.

Long-Term vs. Short-Term Rentals

One of the big advantages of short-term rentals over the traditional long-term rental model, is that it is much more flexible.

With a long-term rental, you become a landlord and will sign a lease with your tenant. Typically, the lease is for one year and you're locked into that agreement for the length of the lease.

However, if you rent out a room or two as an Airbnb host, you can change your mind and turn off your listings whenever you want. You can also adjust your rental rates as peak seasons ebb and flow.

You may think one of the downsides of hosting on Airbnb is the uncertain nature of your revenue. Let's do the "math".

With a long-term lease, you can count on a regular rent check every month. This allows you to budget accordingly, knowing exactly how much money you're going to bring in.

Short-term rentals can be less consistent. However, you can make much more *per night* with STRs. In a good month, there's potential to make two to three times the income you would with a long-term lease.

For example, let's say a long-term rental is rented for $1800/month. That's a nightly rate of $60/night.

For the same house, let's say you rented it on Airbnb with a nightly rate of $160. If you have a perfect month (a fully booked month), that's $4800 for the month!

Needless to say, you can typically count on a higher income from a series of Airbnb guests than from a single tenant.

Host Categories

There are three levels of hosts on Airbnb: ordinary hosts, Superhosts, and Airbnb Plus hosts.

Everyone starts out as an ordinary host. You can be raised to Superhost status if you have a near-perfect rating with great reviews, at least 10 rentals per year, and a low cancellation rate. Superhosts get preferential listing and expedited customer support.

Airbnb Plus hosts are only invited to apply if they are located in select cities across the globe, such as London, New York and Shanghai. To become an Airbnb Plus host, you must pass an in-person inspection with a rigorous checklist of 100 items. And if you don't have a private bathroom for each guest, forget even thinking about it.

While Airbnb Plus status may be beyond your resources and location, you could easily become a Superhost within a few months of starting your business, just like me. It's a worthwhile aim that requires paying attention to the details that will make your guests happy.

Different Airbnb Models

There are several ways to get started with an Airbnb business. One of the ways is to purchase a new property for the sole purpose of renting it out, short term. If this is the way you want to go, you can start your Airbnb business by purchasing a house, townhouse or condominium.

However, if purchasing a property isn't in your budget or plans right now, it's not the only way you can start. There are many other avenues you can take to set up your first Airbnb property.

House Hacking

If you own your own home, house hacking is definitely the easiest way to get started as an Airbnb host. This can also work if you are renting an apartment or townhome with an unused spare room.

As long as you have space in your house to accommodate guests, you can rent out rooms. Maybe you have a bedroom or two sitting empty since the kids moved out, or a den or bonus room that can easily be fitted out as a guest room.

If you have an extra bathroom that can be reserved for the exclusive use of the guests, that's even better.

It also doesn't involve signing leases or putting together a down payment and getting a mortgage for a second property.

In other words, this classic bed and breakfast model is a low-risk way to dip your toes into the STR business.

Rental Arbitrage

Maybe your home is too small to accommodate guests? Or maybe you simply don't have a house to share.

That's where rental arbitrage comes in.

Simply put, this involves you signing a lease on a rental property, and turning that apartment, condo, or house into a STR property.

This doesn't involve a big financial commitment like a mortgage, although you are going to have a monthly rent payment for the duration of the lease.

However, depending on your location and the time of year, you can easily cover your rent check with a couple of weeks of Airbnb guests, and then the rest of the month is pure profit.

Two factors may complicate this approach.

First, your municipality may have regulations regarding subletting a rental property for STRs. Make sure you know what's possible before you sign a lease.

Secondly, the landlord may not be thrilled about an Airbnb being set up in their property. However, you may be able to persuade them that as an Airbnb host, keeping the unit well-maintained and clean is a top priority for your business.

With Rental Arbitrage, any negotiating skills you may have will be a huge asset here. If you're not great at negotiating, it would be wise to brush up on these skills before considering the Rental Arbitrage model.

Glamping
If you own or are considering buying a rural property in a location with natural beauty, Glamping is another way to move into the Airbnb business.

Glamping, or "glamorous camping", is basically taking the "roughing it" out of camping while still having an outdoor-in-the-middle-of-nature experience. This means you can't just set up a common camping tent and start renting it out.

A good quality, higher end tent (which can run more than $2000), is what guests will be looking for. Just because it's higher end doesn't mean it will have all the furnishings and amenities, like heating and electricity.

That means, you will need to come up with your own ways to elevate the camping experience by providing luxuries that are not at a typical camp site. Amenities like bathroom facilities, a mini fridge, and lighting are a few examples.

Remember, the glamorous part of glamping is what makes it such a draw. You can see from listings on Airbnb that hosts go all out to make these experiences as luxurious as possible.

Setting up a few tents or yurts on your land will still cost less than financing a new property or doing extensive renovations.

Co-Hosting

Co-hosting is another model to consider.

There are lots of property owners out there looking for a passive income. They don't want to do all the work that comes with managing an Airbnb, but they do have the money to invest in getting it off the ground.

That's where you can come in and take care of all day-to-day management of their properties. For a cut of the profits (15 to 30%), you manage the bookings, restock supplies, and handle the maintenance and cleaning.

With this model, you can co-host for multiple owners at the same time, turning it into your full-time job. Without having to invest anything upfront, you could easily make more than $5000 a month, depending on how many properties you're managing.

Pros and Cons of Running an Airbnb

Operating an Airbnb business isn't for everyone, but there are a lot of great reasons to become a host. To find out if it's a right move for you, let's weigh the pros and cons of starting an Airbnb business.

First of all, having an Airbnb business provides you with a secondary income stream, even if you're only renting out a spare room in your house. Whether you have a mortgage, or other debts such as student loans to pay off, the money you make as an Airbnb host can help you cover those expenses.

Want to travel more? What about buying a new car? Maybe you could use the extra money to invest in renovations? With a successful Airbnb property, the sky is the limit on how you can spend the extra money you're making.

Then, there is the benefit of taking advantage of tax write-offs for anything connected with your business. This includes everything from coffee and snacks for your guests, to toilet paper, bedding, and even video streaming services.

Most importantly, you will get to be your own boss. This means you will have greater control of your day-to-day. Not only do you get to set your own schedule and have more flexibility of your time, you will also have control over your business and the way it operates.

You get to make the decisions for your business: which model you want to go with, what type of host you want to be, and how to market your business all the way down to the experience you provide to your customers.

On the flip side, think about what will be required of you so you are fully aware of what you're getting into before you get started.

Take into consideration the time commitment of starting and operating an Airbnb business. Think about how you need to obtain a property or space, prepare the property, and manage operations.

Sure, you may choose to contract out some of the daily tasks. In the beginning, I suggest you do them yourself because you will become more familiar with the business this way. With some experience under your feet, you will know how you want things to be done and it will be easier to pass this knowledge on and train others to do things to your standards. All of this, from doing the work yourself, to training someone else to do the work for you, takes time.

Then, you will need to be available to your guests, if only by phone, 24-7. If a toilet overflows at 3 in the morning, it's your problem.

It's not only time that will be spent. It's true you must spend money to make money. For this venture, you will also need some up-front cash to get it off the ground.

Whether you need a down payment on a new property, or new bedding and appliances for your existing space, there are plenty of start-up expenses that must be paid before you greet your first guest.

Finally, in an ideal world, every booking is a success. However, an ideal world is hard to come by and mishaps do happen from time to time.

You may have guests who damage the place, requiring a shut-down of bookings until things are repaired.

Items may go missing from your property or they may break on you. While knickknacks are nice, they are not essential and won't have to be replaced immediately. However, if the microwave or other appliance breaks, those will have to be replaced or repaired as soon as possible.

You may get blowback from neighbors or even law enforcement if guests throw wild parties, even if they don't damage anything.

Some of these issues involve spending money to fix them, while others are more about managing bookings more proactively. Luckily, Airbnb has stepped up on issues like parties, so you shouldn't have to worry as much about them.

Your Mindset Matters

As you prepare for this new adventure, it's important to maintain a positive attitude. Over the course of running your business, you are bound to run into obstacles and challenges. You will need to find ways to stay positive even though sometimes, it may feel like a task.

Maintaining a positive mindset will help you overcome obstacles and help you survive the days that may make you want to give up. Start with a healthy diet and regular exercise. Read positive or inspirational quotes or connect with other Airbnb hosts.

It's helpful to know other hosts because you will be surrounded with like-minded people who go through the same ups and downs as you. Whether you find other hosts on the Airbnb platform, social media or face-to-face, they can be a huge help. Not only will they be there to offer tremendous support when you need it, they will be there during the times on your journey where you feel like you are alone.

Don't get in your own way! It's easy to go down a rabbit hole reading about all the things that can go wrong with your business, excessively watching YouTube videos and over researching this subject to the point where you don't know which way is up or down. This is called "analysis paralysis". How do you stop overanalyzing?

Really, the best way to learn about Airbnb hosting is by jumping in and getting your feet wet.

What if you make mistakes? The truth is mistakes are inevitable. You should embrace your mistakes, be thankful for the lessons they teach you and know they will ultimately shape you into a better host.

While you will probably make some mistakes right off the bat, you will get an on-the-job training that can't be found in any book, even this one.

For instance, don't let a bad review spoil your day. Yes, it's easy to get discouraged when you feel like you are being criticized, but there are a couple of things you can do to move past it.

First, look at all your positive reviews to gain some perspective. Remember, you provided a place for people to enjoy themselves, reconnect with loved ones, or find a welcoming place to spend a night.

Then, go back to that negative review and make it a learning experience. See if there's anything in there you can learn from to improve your Airbnb game in the future.

Another way to keep a positive mindset is to pay attention to and celebrate the small "wins" you will have. Obviously, your Airbnb business isn't going to grow overnight. Think of starting your business as a journey with small milestones, or "wins", along the way until it has grown into what you want it to be.

Celebrating these wins will allow you to stop and reflect on what you have accomplished so far. This will help you keep the momentum of positivity going.

You can also always go back to your "why" whenever you are in doubt. This powerful statement will help you remember why this journey is so important to you, to begin with.

If you keep a positive attitude and don't let an obstacle stay in your way, you have what it takes to succeed. My advice to you is this: stop over analyzing and if you're going to do this business – start NOW!

Action Items to DO NOW!:

1. Define Your "Why?"
The first thing you need to do is have a clear understanding of "why" you are choosing to build an Airbnb business (your reason, your motivation, your inspiration). Then, write it down and post it somewhere you will see it, regularly.

2. Commit to Learning the Business
Make a commitment to yourself to learn what you need to know to get your business off the ground, to always learn from your mistakes and commit to excel in your business every step of the way.

3. Keep a Positive Attitude
Commit to yourself that you are going to be a great Airbnb host and go into this with a positive outlook. Promise yourself you won't get bogged down with all the "what if's" or disaster scenarios. Know you can do this and there is nothing that can stop you!

Chapter Two

Your Airbnb Business Explained

O nce you decide which type of business model you would like to move forward with, it's time to consider the various expenses you will have. These expenses will fall into two fairly distinct categories: initial start-up costs and ongoing expenses. Let's look at both of these separately.

The Associated Costs of an Airbnb Business

Start-Up Costs

Before you even think about putting your listing up on Airbnb, you need to sink a fair amount of money into getting your new enterprise off the ground.

If you don't have a suitable place to start hosting guests, you will have to either purchase a property or rent an apartment or house. Whether it's a mortgage down payment or first and last month's rent and security deposit, you need to have the cash on hand to cover those costs.

The funds used for a new location is not the only expense you will have. You still need funds to furnish the space and fit it out with all the necessities your guests will expect to find.

Necessities like furniture, appliances, bedding, kitchen supplies such as pots, pans, and plates, and even streaming service subscriptions. Don't forget decorative details, either. Spending money on striking artwork and decor can help make your listing stand out from the crowd.

Also, investing money in new outdoor furnishings will increase the appeal of your listing. Maybe you want to offer amenities like a hot tub or a fire pit? Or maybe you need to build a deck to create your outdoor space? If you already have the deck in place, what will you need to purchase to create the setting?

If you are simply planning to rent out a couple of rooms in your own home, you may be lucky to already have furniture in place, but don't settle for old and okay. If your bedroom or common room furniture is showing signs of wear and tear, you should replace it before you welcome guests to your home.

Additionally, seriously consider the condition of your guest bathroom. The expense of a new toilet or tub to replace fixtures that are showing their age will pay off in good reviews.

Depending on how much you have on hand, furnishing an empty house or apartment can easily end up costing you several thousands of dollars. Even a one-bedroom apartment could cost more than $6,000 to set up, while a two-bedroom condo might run over $10,000 to be properly equipped.

Remember, it's the photographs in your listing that will bring the first customers to your new Airbnb. The better the place looks, the more likely you are to get bookings quickly.

Ongoing Expenses
Of course, you're not finished when your first guests walk through the door. You will need to keep spending money on recurring expenses such as monthly rent or mortgage payments, insurance, and utilities.

There's also the cost of washing bedding and towels and cleaning the entire space between every rental. This means there are supplies that need to be purchased, and the cost of water, gas, and electricity to be factored in.

Guests will also go through items such as soap and other toiletries, paper products, and coffee and tea.

Additionally, if you're planning to operate a traditional bed-and-breakfast and will serve breakfast to your guests, you will need to buy essentials like bacon, eggs, bread, and other breakfast items on a regular basis.

Also, assume you will have to replace bedding and towels over time, as they get used. Your whites will get dingy and sometimes items will just disappear. Replenishing inventory is an ongoing expense.

Luckily, by the time you need to restock, you will have some income coming in from your bookings, but it's best to budget ahead anyway.

Business Structure

Whether your Airbnb is a room or two in your home, or a large portfolio of apartments, houses, and cottages, it's best to keep your business finances separate from your personal finances.

Start by registering your business as a Limited Liability Company (LLC). This protects your personal assets from any legal actions taken against your Airbnb. Another advantage of setting up an LLC is you may be able to get a mortgage for an income property through the LLC rather than on your personal credit. As time goes on and you build up a good credit rating for your business, that becomes an asset when you want to borrow money down the road.

Check with an attorney and your mortgage company to see what the rules are regarding the purchase of a property through an LLC.

Next, set up a separate bank account for your revenue and expenses. Have a separate debit card and credit card for your business and use it for all expenditures related to the Airbnb business, and nothing else.

If you are operating your Airbnb in a separate location from your home, use the new business account to pay the rent, mortgage, and utilities on that property, as well as all supplies and associated expenses.

Research Local Laws

The time to find out what the local laws are regarding Airbnbs is not after you have opened your door to guests.

In fact, you need to do this research before you even put in an offer on a property or sign a lease. You may learn that the business model you have in mind is simply not possible in the location that you were planning to operate in.

Some cities have placed strict limitations on Airbnbs, citing concerns about the lack of long-term rental space, and disruptive activity such as parties interfering with residents. These include such tourist meccas as Orlando and Las Vegas.

Many municipalities limit the number of days a year that hosts can rent out accommodation.

Others, including New York City, do not permit renting out an entire space for less than 30 days. The only permitted STRs are where rooms in a home are rented out by a host who also lives there. Obviously, that makes it impossible to build up a portfolio of Airbnb properties.

Many cities, such as Chicago and San Francisco, have instituted an occupancy tax which is payable to the municipality on an ongoing basis.

Even rural municipalities with popular vacation destinations are looking at limiting the number or type of Airbnb accommodations permitted in their area. Many towns and cities will require an Airbnb to be licensed, which may entail inspections in addition to annual fees.

The restrictions on Airbnbs do not mean it's impossible to find a location to start your business.

This simply means you have to do some preliminary work before you fully commit and check out the regulations regarding STRs in your city or town.

Do not assume you can fly under the radar and list your property, anyway. This is NOT a case where it is better to ask for forgiveness rather than permission. You may find yourself on the hook for substantial fines if you get caught.

In fact, even if you are planning to rent out rooms in your home in a community that's part of a Homeowners Association (HOA) or in your condominium, you may have to obtain permission from the board before proceeding with your plans. Having a STR set up is not an activity that's typically allowed and it won't be easy to hide from neighbors, so take care of any issues like this ahead of time.

Furthermore, do not assume that the current laws in your jurisdiction will not change over time because this is still a very new business model.

As an Airbnb host, you should stay informed about new regulations that may be introduced that could affect your ability to continue to operate your business.

Taxes for Your Airbnb Property

Once you've opened for business and are earning income from your Airbnb, you will need to file a federal tax return and pay taxes on that income. However, there are other taxes you may be liable to pay as well.

Federal and State Income Taxes

In the United States, if you earn more than $600 in a year, Airbnb will send you a Form 1099-K, as well as report it to the IRS and your state revenue agency.

However, as an Airbnb owner, you have potential deductions you can use to lower the amount of taxes you have to pay.

This can include mortgage or rent payments, utilities, insurance, and supplies used in the Airbnb. If you hire a cleaner or maintenance person, don't pay them under the table, as you will want to claim their fees as well.

If you are renting out rooms in your own home, those expenses will be pro-rated to the proportion of the property that is used for guests, as well as the frequency that it is occupied.

Capital expenses such as furnishings and repairs or renovations can also be used to lighten your tax bill.

Make sure you always keep the receipts from all purchases related to your Airbnb business throughout the year so you can claim everything possible. You may find a receipt scanner or app a worthwhile investment to streamline the process.

It's also a good idea to hire an accountant to prepare your tax return. Unless you're a real expert in this area, a professional will best be able to find all the deductions you're entitled to.

Sales Tax

In some municipalities, you will be required to assess and collect sales tax from your guests, just as a hotel would have to do.

In many jurisdictions, Airbnb does this automatically as part of the reservation fee, so you don't have to worry about it on your end.

You can add any additional taxes to your daily rate if it is not currently automatically collected by Airbnb.

Insurance

Think of the potential damage that could arise from hosting guests, especially if you're not on the premises. Therefore, you will need to ensure that your Airbnb is fully insured. First, know that simply having your business set up as an LLC will not protect you, fully.

This is why liability insurance is very important. If a guest sustains an injury while on your property, for instance, you will need coverage if you are sued.

Also, Airbnb provides hosts with some insurance coverage, yet it is strongly recommended you purchase additional insurance to protect yourself and your business more fully.

AirCover

When you become an Airbnb host, you are automatically enrolled in AirCover for Hosts as soon as you list a property on their site. This also means you will have some coverage for every booking.

AirCover offers host liability insurance and host damage protection of $1,000,000 each.

Host liability insurance covers any issue where a guest has been injured or their property has been damaged or stolen, while staying at your Airbnb.

This can include bodily injury, theft, or damage of property. It can also include damage by the guest to building common areas (such as an apartment lobby) or nearby properties.

However, it does not include assault and battery, communicable disease, damage, or injury from deliberate actions (as opposed to accidental) among other exclusions.

Host damage protection covers any damage to your property caused by an Airbnb guest.

This includes damage to the building or belongings, including furnishings and appliances, unexpected cleaning expenses as a result of guest activity, and lost host income if you have to cancel bookings to deal with the above issues.

It does not include normal wear and tear or damage resulting from natural disasters such as hurricanes or earthquakes.

You would only receive a payout from this policy after attempting to obtain reimbursement from the guest. You must submit a request for reimbursement within 14 days of the responsible guest checking out.

Airbnb Support will work with you to get payment from the guest. If that fails, you may get paid through the host damage protection.

Additional Insurance
Do not count on the Airbnb insurance coverage to be enough in case of issues arising from running a STR business.

Luckily, there are lots of insurance companies out there that now offer additional insurance tailored to Airbnb hosts.

Start by getting in touch with your current insurance broker, as they will be able to look around and find the best policy for your situation. If you know other Airbnb hosts in your area, it's also a good idea to check in with them and find out what insurance coverage they have, and through which company.

Definitely lock this down before you start hosting guests as you don't want any nasty surprises down the road.

Budgeting and Planning

Before you start spending money establishing your Airbnb business, you will want to set up a budget.

It's too easy to get carried away and make some extravagant purchases when a little advance planning will help you keep your expenses in line. When creating your budget, it should reflect the size of your space, the amount of furniture that needs to be purchased upfront, and any renovations that need to be completed. For instance, the amount of money you will need to acquire and furnish a three-bedroom house will differ from the amount of money you will need for a one-bedroom apartment. Therefore, you need to set your limits because if you're not paying attention, purchases can add up, quickly.

If you have a one-bedroom apartment to furnish, you should try to stay between $5,000 and $6,000 dollars. A two-bedroom might run as high as $10,000, depending on how high-end you want to go. Planning to rent out an entire house? You will pay a lot more. This is why you need to budget accordingly. Give yourself a strict limit and stay within it.

Start with how much you feel comfortable investing in order to acquire a property. Know what you can manage for either a mortgage or monthly rental payments. Assume you will need to make at least one to three payments before you can start hosting guests.

When it comes to a down payment, don't stretch yourself to your very limit. You will still have to spend money to get the place ready before you can turn around and start renting it out.

When furnishing your space, don't overspend to get set up if you can't realistically see getting it back soon. Make sure you prioritize the things you "must" buy before you spend your budget on art and other non-essentials. You can always add the extras as time goes on, but first, spend your money on the things that will ensure a comfortable stay for your guests.

If you're tight on cash, it doesn't hurt to purchase some items in advance before you put in an offer or sign a lease. Giving yourself a longer time frame to acquire items can take off a lot of pressure and you may even be able to take advantage of sales.

If you can save a few hundred dollars apiece on appliances or furniture, or pick up bedding on sale, that can really help your budget down the road.

Also remember, from the moment you take possession of your Airbnb property, you're paying utilities, insurance, and taxes. Make sure to include these figures into your budget, as well.

Create Your Plan: Your Dream Airbnb Situation

It's time to get your plan down on paper. Now that you know what to expect as an Airbnb host, you should be able to make some basic decisions about how to move forward with making this dream a reality.

While there are always going to be bumps in the road that require modifications to your plan, you won't be able to set out on this journey without a map to guide you. Let's start with the basics.

What Type of Property Do You Want to Have?

One of the first things you need to do when starting to plan, is to choose which business model you want to pursue. Look back at Chapter 1 to review the different Airbnb Models (buying a property, House Hacking, Arbitrage, Glamping or Co-Hosting) and make this decision before you go any further.

Do you want to start with renting out rooms in your own home?

Would you prefer to rent a separate apartment or condo to host guests?

Or do you want to purchase an entire house to rent out?

While the standard units of individual bedrooms in a house or full apartments, townhomes, or houses are well-established options, you could also go for more unique units.

For some inspiration on what unique stays look like, go to Airbnb and click on the "OMG!" icon. You'll find hobbit houses, railway carriages, and treehouses, among many other unique STR properties.

I don't expect you to aim for that degree of uniqueness in your first Airbnb, but it should help you understand that developing a property that stands out from the pack will increase your chances for success.

Some hosts have even taken vintage trailers and completely renovated them, creating charming small spaces that can easily be set up in a small city backyard. Others have built tiny homes on their property.

If a unique stay is not for you, perhaps buying rural acreage for a glamping site sounds more appealing? As discussed previously, Glamping is a growing sector of the Airbnb market. Cottages, of course, have long been popular Airbnb destinations.

You can be as creative as you want. Think about your ideal situation and what you want your property to be, look and feel like, and write it down.

Who Are Your Guests?
Not all Airbnbs, or all locations, appeal to all audiences. It's up to you to do your research so you can more effectively market yourself to likely guests.

The easiest locations for pinpointing likely guest demographics are vacation spots.

For instance, if you are located in or near a busy beach resort, you can expect most guests to be beachgoers.

They will be looking for amenities that match with that destination, such as a hot tub or pool.

On the other hand, if you are planning to locate in a major city, your guests could be visiting for any number of reasons.

For example, a business traveler may need a dedicated workspace with excellent Wi-Fi and families may need kid-friendly accommodations for their children. Other visitors could be regular tourists looking to take in the sights and want a knowledgeable host to guide their visit.

Consider these factors when deciding on the type of property to purchase and how to set it up. When it comes time to market your property, you will also use this information to attract certain types of guests who you suspect will be staying at your STR.

How Much Would You Like to Earn Each Month?

By now, you should have a decent understanding of the initial costs associated with your Airbnb business. But, let's be honest, you are planning to become an Airbnb host to make money.

How much money do you want to make each month? Every year? Here's where you need to make an educated estimate on potential income. Be realistic.

To make sure you're not taking a stab in the dark, check out how other Airbnbs in your area are doing. Use a site like AirDNA to give you current daily rates, occupancy percentages, and estimated monthly revenues for your location and property type. Then, use these results to base your expectations on.

Set achievable goals for your monthly and yearly revenue. Then, commit to working towards those numbers. You may find in your research that revenues vary seasonally, and you have to account for that as well in your plan. Once you've crunched the numbers, you will know how much you can afford to spend on setting up your Airbnb.

Think about the costs associated with your property. Are the income numbers you see enough to cover the costs in your budget we identified earlier? Part of your plan should be to recoup your startup costs within the first four months of operation.

Where Do You See Yourself in Five Years?
What do you want your business to look like five years down the road?

You may want to keep this as a side gig and only have one or two properties, or just continue to rent out the rooms in your home.

Or maybe your dream is bigger? You can turn this into a full-time job and make a very comfortable living with multiple properties.

Once you've determined your five-year goal, set up interim milestones to help you achieve it. Where should you be in one year? In three? These smaller milestones should help take you down the path to get closer to, and achieve, your five-year goal.

Make Your Goals SMART

It's always a good practice to write down your goals. I recommend making your goals "SMART" to clarify exactly what you're trying to achieve with your Airbnb business. Then, you can create a vision statement that will serve as inspiration to make your vision a reality.

When writing out your goals for the vision of your Airbnb business, the more descriptive they are, the better. You can do this by homing in on the details of your goal to be Specific, Measurable, Achievable, Realistic, and Timely (SMART). These SMART Goals will set you up for success by giving you a sense of direction whenever you feel lost on your Airbnb journey.

Specific: Instead of saying, "I want to make extra money from my Airbnb", use specifics to outline *what you want* to accomplish.

Measurable: You will need to be able to determine your progress by measuring your actual performance in real time compared to your goal. For example, you can set an objective for exactly *how much* extra money you want to make over a period of time.

Achievable: Obviously, you want to set yourself up for success. At the same time you also want to push yourself a little outside your comfort level. Make sure your goal challenges you a bit but is still possible for you to achieve.

Realistic: I'm not against "shooting for the stars", but while your goal should be able to challenge you and stretch you a little, make sure it's something you can easily reach. Do not try to overextend yourself with unrealistic goals that will end up hurting you more than helping you.

Timely: Give yourself a deadline to hit your goal by.

Here's an example:
I will make an extra $3000 profit per month by owning a three-bedroom home in the Outer Banks, North Carolina, that will be set up for families who want to spend time at the beach, within 12 months of listing my first property.

Consider the difference between that and something like:

I will open an Airbnb and make some extra income.

The first one will make it much easier to focus on reaching the level of success you want!

Action Items to DO NOW!:

1. Get Your Finances in Order
Set up a bank account and debit and credit cards to make sure your business revenue and expenses are separate from your personal ones.

2. Check to See If There Are Any Laws or Restrictions Where You Plan to Have An Airbnb Property
Do your research! Don't just assume you will be okay because the consequences of not following the rules can be expensive.

3. Figure Out Your Costs and Set Your Budget
Make a list of all the costs that will be associated with your Airbnb business, including what you can expect to pay to acquire a property and set it up.
Also, use AirDNA to see what others in your area are making and create a realistic budget based off of your findings.

4. Create Your Plan and Set Your Goals
Make a plan that outlines the details of your business. Who are your guests? How much do you want to earn each month? Where do you see yourself in five years?

5. Define your SMART Goal

Make sure it's Specific, Measurable, Achievable, Realistic, and Timely (SMART).

Here's a template to get you started:

I will make [amount of money in terms of profit, revenue, income, etc.] per [week, month, year, etc.] by owning a [type of property], in [location] that will be set up for [type of guests] to [activity or reason they will stay at your property] in [amount of time].

Chapter Three

Finding Your Ideal Property

W hile I know you are eager to move forward with this exciting new venture, you don't want to make a hasty purchase you may later regret. Therefore, we are going to focus on doing the due diligence required to feel confident your new property is right for you.

What Makes a Good Airbnb Location?

If you have made the decision to acquire a property, separate from your home, it's time to start searching for a place to rent or purchase.

This shouldn't be a snap decision. There are a lot of factors to consider before committing yourself to the purchase or lease of a space to turn into a STR.

Your search should start with looking into the best location.

When searching for the ideal location for your Airbnb, there are some important considerations to take into account.

It's time to sit down at your computer and dig into the details.

Start by making a list of preferred areas so you're not overwhelmed by too many options. Use the following key criteria when drawing it up.

Stay Close to Home

Since you're not looking for a home for yourself, you don't have the same limitations of work location or family obligations that would otherwise limit your options. Given this freedom, you can look further away than your typical commute.

However, for your first Airbnb property, even though you will be learning how to develop a team close to the Airbnb to take care of essentials like routine cleaning and property maintenance, I strongly recommend you don't venture too far from home.

This is because you can expect this first foray into STR hosting to have a bit of a learning curve and you will benefit from not having to travel too far if an emergency arises at your Airbnb property.

Another big advantage of staying in your own town or city is you will already be very familiar with the area, including visitor attractions, good restaurants, and even the sections of town with the lowest crime rates.

This doesn't mean you have to buy a place right down the street from your own home, or even in the same town. A place within one to four hours away is still close enough to make the trip out to the rental when necessary.

Choose a Place You Like

Consider your own preferences when choosing where to set up your Airbnb. After all, why should your property only be used for your guests? You may want to (and should) stay there once in a while, too.

You probably have a favorite getaway destination. For some of you, it might be a mountain community, or a lake or oceanside resort. Maybe you have a city you like to visit for its nightlife, shopping, or sports.

Whatever your preference, a place you can use as your own vacation home occasionally, is a great place to purchase your first Airbnb property.

While you won't be making money when you book it for yourself, you won't have to pay for accommodations, either.

Down to the Details

Once you have your short list of potential locations, it's time to really zero in on the important factors to see which one makes the final cut. Ask Yourself:

Why Do People Visit This Place?
Not every location draws visitors for the same reasons. For instance, people visit Zion National Park to go hiking, travel to Aspen for skiing, or visit Hilton Head to enjoy the beach.

In a major city, there are various reasons why travelers need STR accommodation. They might be ordinary tourists who want to take in the sights, but they could also be on a business trip, or need to spend some time near a major hospital while a loved one is being treated.

Consider all these possibilities when deciding on the best place to set up your Airbnb.

What Are the Local Rules and Regulations?
Before you get too excited about any one location, you need to know if your STR model is even possible in that jurisdiction. With some locations there may be limitations on the number of nights a year you can host, while others require the host to be living in the building. Others do not allow STRs at all.

For instance, people visit Orlando to go to Disney World. However, Orlando has very tight restrictions on STRs. This means you should look to nearby towns, like Kissimmee, that are more lenient.

Make sure you check the local rules and regulations of the property you are considering to make sure there are no limitations.

What About the Taxes?

While federal income tax can be expected to be constant across the whole country, state taxes will vary and individual cities may levy additional surcharges on STRs, too.

In many jurisdictions Airbnb collects and pays these taxes directly, otherwise, you are responsible for remitting them to your city. Again, make sure you do your research on the taxes that you will need to pay in the location you're considering.

Don't let high or additional taxes scare you if you are scouting a location in a high occupancy destination. It's likely that higher revenues will offset any additional taxes you may have to pay.

Consult an accountant on the best way to handle taxes with your specific situation.

What's the Local Economy Like?

You should look for a spot with a strong local economy when selecting your Airbnb location.

A city with a growing tax base will be able to invest more money into the amenities that will attract visitors, such as public transportation, parks and museums.

On the other hand, a city with lots of boarded-up buildings and run-down streets simply won't be as appealing to tourists.

Is the Location Safe?

People don't want to visit a place unless they can feel safe.

Investigate the crime statistics for the city or town and if possible, for different parts of the same community. This can help you focus on which part of the city you should look for a property.

If you're not sure where to look, websites such as bestplaces.net and city-data.com can help.

Is There Potential for Natural Disasters?

Unfortunately, certain regions are simply more likely to experience a natural disaster. The most obvious example are hurricanes, which annually inflict a considerable amount of damage on coastal communities.

If you have a property in one of these areas, you may not be able to get flood insurance to cover damage. Also keep in mind, government assistance is often limited to principal residences rather than income properties.

While there's no way to predict exactly where hurricanes will make landfall in any given year, or how strong they will be, it's a fact the Atlantic and Gulf Coasts are particularly at risk.

However, these same Coasts are extremely popular vacation destinations, making an Airbnb there a potential goldmine.

You will need to weigh the risk to reward ratio for your situation. Some have a stronger stomach for higher risk, while others don't want to deal with it at all.

Check Out Your Competitors

Your research should also include other Airbnbs in the area you're thinking of setting up shop in. It's as simple as searching for current STRs using the Airbnb site.

Checking out other vacation rental properties in the region can give you a sense of what you should be aiming for. Realize you're not necessarily looking to duplicate the same model you see most commonly listed. Instead, be on the lookout for an untapped niche you can move into.

However, the likelihood is if a certain type of STR predominates in an area, it's because that is what people are looking for.

Start by searching for the city or region you're considering and scroll through what's currently available. If you already have a specific neighborhood or street in mind, you can narrow it down to that. Then, select 10 listings, and start to analyze what makes them work so well (or not).

Is the Market Oversaturated?

This is one of the most infamous questions that is asked about Airbnb. The answer is: it depends. You will need to do some research to find missed opportunities in the area you're considering.

Looking at the availability for the various listings will help you determine if the market for a certain property type has been saturated yet and whether you should branch off in a different direction.

Here's a good way to figure out if a specific location has room for more Airbnbs or if there is untapped potential you can take advantage of.

First, establish a relatively small area with a high number of potential draws for visitors. This can include venues like sports arenas, concert halls and convention centers for tourists, office districts for business travelers, or nearby hospitals and medical centers.

Then, select last-minute stays for two or three people and see what's there.

If there are plenty of good listings still available, this is an indication that the demand in this area is low. Therefore, you should consider changing the focus of your property search to different locations or different types of properties in the same location.

On the other hand, if all that comes up are STRs with poor or few reviews, low-quality photos and few amenities, you probably can move into that market with a fair potential for success. In this case, your goal would be to make your property better than the other properties in the area.

The types of properties that predominate in a specific market will obviously vary depending on the location. For instance, apartment rentals are popular in cities because visitors are typically not looking for outdoor amenities. On the other hand, a popular hiking destination will no doubt have plenty of cabins and vacation homes listed on Airbnb.

However, moving out of those comfort zones a bit may pay off by appealing to a different audience. For example, in a beach town, some people may not want to spend the money to rent an entire space for a couple of days when they will barely be at the house. Instead, you could consider setting up a house with several bedrooms to rent out separately, with shared common spaces and kitchen.

In a city, some visitors need a larger space than a one or two-bedroom apartment. Investing in a four-bedroom home will appeal to guests traveling in a larger group.

What do the Amenities look like?
Look at which amenities are being offered at other properties since those are the things guests will then expect in your Airbnb.

For instance, if most of the listings feature a hot tub or swimming pool, that means they are likely to be more attractive to potential guests in that area. If current listings have king-sized beds and luxury showers, you probably aren't going to get very far with double beds and a standard bathtub.

One reason guests may favor a vacation rental property over a standard hotel room is the kitchen. If the other properties available in your preferred location have shiny new kitchens with high-quality appliances, that's something you will need to offer as well.

How Do Others Price Their Properties?

It is important to pay attention to the rates charged by other Airbnbs already operating in your target location. While there may be some variation between the different STR properties, you should start to get a feel for the average rates the local market will bear.

Successful Airbnb operators pay close attention to the trends in rates for their area, which can fluctuate considerably throughout the year. For instance, in a northern lakeside resort town, an Airbnb host can charge much more at the height of the summer season than in the depths of winter.

On the other hand, a STR in a city can probably expect a more consistent revenue stream throughout the year.

Don't base an estimate of annual revenue on just a month or two, as that may result in an under or over-valuing of the potential of that location.

What Are the Reviews Telling You?

Reviews are a great way to gauge what guests value most in an Airbnb property.

First, a property that doesn't have a lot of reviews may be an indication it fell short of guest expectations.

It's worth taking a few minutes to scroll through the listing to see what may have triggered that lack of response so you know what to avoid.

Next, pay attention to negative reviews as they can contain valuable clues to what you, as a good host, will be expected to provide.

Of course, glowing 5-star reviews can be a goldmine of information for your own Airbnb.

While not all guests have the same preferences, you should be able to draw conclusions about which characteristics of an Airbnb are most desirable for visitors to that location.

Time To Find a Property

By now you should have pinpointed a specific location for your first Airbnb.

Now, it's time to find a property and make an offer on it. If you have ever used real estate websites such as Redfin or Zillow, you know how easy it is to get started on your search for a property.

First, select your preferred city or region. Then, restrict your search to preferred home types, number of beds and baths, and price.

You can even draw a boundary to get a custom list of properties without having to sift through a huge geographical region to find what you want. That's particularly helpful if you're looking to focus on a specific draw such as an arena or business district.

Use these tools to narrow down your list of potential properties before you even get in the car to check things out in person.

Property Type

After doing your research on which property types predominate in your chosen location, you should have a good idea of what will work best for you.

Remember, if the current listings in this area are usually fully booked, you can be confident you can enter the market with a similar property and have a good occupancy rate.

However, if you've found this area has a limited inventory of other property types, you could be able to fill that gap by going with a different type of property.

For instance, if there are lots of listings for two-bedroom apartments, maybe you could branch out with a studio apartment that's perfect for short stays for one or two people? Or you could go in the other direction and buy a three-bedroom house that would work better for a family on a week's vacation.

Try looking for a few different property types in your preferred area and see what's available at a reasonable price before making a final decision.

Property Condition

Even without visiting the property, you should be able to get a good idea of what its current condition is. This will help you determine how much time and money you will have to spend to get it ready to rent out.

For instance, if the walls are covered with dated wallpaper, you are going to have to invest your own labor or pay for someone else to strip it off and repaint. The same goes for vinyl floors or carpets that are past their best.

Similarly, if the kitchen or bathrooms are hopelessly outdated you probably won't be able to get away with just a cosmetic update and will have to spend a fair amount on bringing them into the 21st century.

If you're looking at a house that currently has a lot of garden beds and other outdoor features, the cost of landscaping must be factored into your start-up costs.

Those costs, however, will be nothing compared to what's required for putting on a new roof, repairing foundations, installing a new HVAC system, or re-siding the exterior walls.

Plus, any remodeling or construction projects you need will add on to the length of time before you can open for business.

While a house might look like a great bargain, if the cost of fixing it up before listing it on Airbnb is too high, you're better off striking it from your list.

Personally, I prefer houses that don't need a lot of updates because you don't need to budget much for renovations. If you can find a turnkey house, that will be your best bet.

Run the Numbers

When you find a property you think has potential to become your new Airbnb, you need to look at the numbers to see if it will be a worthwhile investment.

You can use programs like AirDNA and AllTheRooms to get some insight into how much money you can make with a specific property. For this example, I will be referencing AirDNA, but you can use whichever platform you prefer.

First, go to AirDNA and enter the address of the property you're looking to purchase in the search bar. You will then see a projection of the potential annual revenue, the average daily rate and what you can expect your occupancy rate to look like.

Once you have all the data for this property, it is a good idea to verify the numbers AirDNA provided. Go to Airbnb to do some more research on what your competitors are bringing in and to see if the numbers from AirDNA line up.

Start by doing an open search (don't enter any dates) in the area the property is in. This will give you everything available in that area. Using the map area feature, try to get as close to the location of your property as possible. Then, start scrolling through listings to find similar properties to the one you are looking at.

After you have found a few, take note of the rates they are charging. Change the dates a few times to see if the rates change. If the rates change, take the average of the different values.

Next, look at their availability over the next couple of months. Does it align with the occupancy rate AirDNA provided? You don't have to get an exact rate of your competitor's properties, but you should be able to eyeball it and come close. For example, if your competitor is booked 20 days next month, that is about a 66% (20/30= 66%) occupancy rate.

Repeat this for a couple of other competitor properties. Once you have all the competitor data, compare it with the AirDNA data for your property. If your competitor research shows they are doing better than what AirDNA projects for your property, it is likely you can do better, too. If their numbers are worse, it might be worth looking at a different property.

If you are happy with the estimates from AirDNA, plug those figures into your budget. Update the expenses for this property in your budget as well. The real estate websites like Redfin or Zillow have calculators that will display what your estimated monthly insurance, taxes and mortgage expense will be.

What's your budget telling you? Will you be set up to make money with this property?

Here's how to tell:
Figure out your potential monthly revenue by dividing the annual rate by 12.

Then, subtract your monthly expenses from this number to get your estimated monthly profit.

When looking at your estimated monthly profit, you don't want the number to be "0" because that will mean you are breaking even and making back your money. That's it. Nothing more.

You also don't want this number to be negative because it means you will lose money each month.

What you're looking for is a healthy positive number. Meaning, you want the number to be positive, but you want it to be well above your breakeven point. This means you will be making some profit.

When you have a property that is showing healthy profit, the final step is to compare your estimated monthly profit with the goals you set. Do these numbers align? If so, it's safe to say you can move forward and purchase this property.

Action Items to DO NOW!:

1. Choose a Location
Make a short list of preferred locations for your first Airbnb. Either start close to home or in a vacation spot you know and love to visit. There's no reason why your Airbnb can't also be your vacation getaway.

2. Conduct Market Research
Sit down at your computer and find out all you can about your preferred locations. Know why people would be visiting. Inform yourself about local laws and taxes. Ensure the local economy is in good shape and the crime rate is low. Also, make sure the risk for natural disasters is something you can handle.

3. Research the Competition
Find other Airbnb listings in your preferred location to see what's already available. Find out what guests value in an Airbnb in those places to better choose a winning property.

4. Find a Property
Using real estate sites such as Redfin or Zillow, find the property type you want in the location you've decided on. Ensure it's in good enough condition to be fixed up and listed, quickly and will be easy to clean and maintain for your guests.

5. Run the Numbers on Potential Properties
Use Airbnb and sites like AirDNA with your budget, to figure out if the property you found will give you enough income to make a profit.

6. Purchase Your Property
Once you've done all your due diligence, move forward to acquire the property.

CHAPTER FOUR

Making Your Property "Guest Ready"

Whether you have purchased your property already or are in the process of the purchase, you can now move forward to work on setting up your Airbnb.

Once your offer is accepted, you will have some time, whether it's a few weeks or a couple of months before you take possession. Use this time for planning so you can hit the ground running when you are handed the keys.

When you have the keys to your property, realize you are now under a time constraint. Each day you spend fixing up your property for guests is one less day you're actually renting it out and making money.

First, let's assume the property is in pretty good shape and all you need to do are cosmetic upgrades, rather than structural. Aim to get everything set up and ready to go a week or two after you're into the property.

If you have renovations or construction projects to take care of first, make sure you work with your contractors on a project plan with a deadline that works with your budget.

Remember, time is money and the planning you do in advance will make it possible to meet your tight set-up schedule.

What Makes a Great Guest Experience?

Providing guests with a positive experience will lead to more bookings and 5-star reviews. This leaves you with the task of creating an Airbnb that will attract guests and give them the best experience possible before, during and after their stay.

In fact, your business should revolve around the experience you provide to guests. From the moment they see your listing, the communications they have with you, all the way until they leave your property, you have the opportunity to leave a positive lasting impression on them.

Realize that one of the reasons people are drawn to Airbnb is for the experience. If all they want is a convenient place to sleep, they can get that at a hotel. With your Airbnb, give your guests more than a place to stay that will delight and intrigue them.

To find out what sort of experience guests are looking for, it's important to understand what they value in an Airbnb. Earlier, I advised you to look at reviews for similar properties to help you figure this out. Now that you have your house, it's a good time to revisit them.

Make a list of the things they feel drawn to comment on, either positively or negatively, as part of your planning process for your own property. Not only will this help you discover what guests expect from properties in your area, but also what they feel is lacking.

Knowing this information gives you the opportunity to fill those gaps. In other words, if you can deliver both the amenities offered by other properties as well as those they don't have, your Airbnb will have a competitive edge.

Amenities

Amenities are the features your Airbnb offers that guests can take advantage of during their stay. For example, Wi-Fi, dedicated workspace, indoor fireplace, dishwasher, lake access, climbing wall (yes, that is a possible amenity!), and the list goes on.

Remember, the amenities you have at your property can help differentiate you from other Airbnbs in your area. For instance, if you have a hot tub and only a few others do, that will give your property extra appeal.

You will see when we talk about creating your listing in the next chapter, Airbnb provides a checklist for you to mark the amenities in your space. Don't get overwhelmed by the sheer volume of the options they list. You are not obligated to have them all. Simply take a good look at your new property and figure out which unique features it already has.

Housekeeping

A clean Airbnb is not an option. This is the most important component of your operation and should be planned out and executed at the highest level.

You will need to hire a cleaner at some point, but you should really start out cleaning the place yourself at first, if possible. Cleaning yourself will allow you to establish what your expectations of cleanliness will be. Knowing exactly how and what to clean will also make it easier when you are training your cleaning crew.

After you have personally cleaned a few times, you will want to pass this duty off to a professional cleaner - unless cleaning is a passion of yours. While you won't need cleaning staff until you're hosting guests, you will want to line them up well before they are needed. Good cleaners are in high demand and finding the right one may take some time.

You have a couple of options when hiring cleaning staff: either one individual or a housekeeping service.

Many hosts choose to go with one person, especially if their property isn't in a major city where professional cleaning services are more likely to be found.

Also, when you work with an independent cleaner, their fees may be lower because you are paying them for the cleaning service, only. Plus, you can be confident they know your expectations for your property because you will work with them over and over.

On the flip side, a professional cleaning service may end up being more expensive than an individual cleaner. This is because the cleaning services add their own fees on top of what they pay the cleaning staff. Another thing to note is you may never have the same person cleaning your place every time.

However, what happens if your independent cleaner gets sick? Or wants a week or two off to go on vacation? You may find yourself scrambling to find a replacement at short notice or end up doing the work yourself.

Hiring a professional cleaning service will eliminate that issue. They will be able to switch in another employee to take over in case of an emergency which could make up for the additional costs. They will also already have a clearly established cleaning protocol to ensure that everything is taken care of between rentals.

If you need help finding cleaners TurnoverBnB will help you find cleaners and automate scheduling and payment. Taskrabbit and Thumbtack will both help connect you with local cleaners.

You can obviously make the choice that is right for you and your business. Whichever option you go with, don't settle for the first one you talk to. After doing your research, interview three candidates and hire the best as soon as possible.

One last important thing to consider in terms of cleaning is setting up an owner's or housekeeping closet in your Airbnb. We'll go into more detail about this in Chapter 6 – right now, you should make sure you have a space reserved for it.

Safety and Security

Obviously, ensuring the safety of your guests should be paramount in your planning, too. With that said, there are a few necessary safety devices you must provide in your Airbnb.

By now everyone should be aware of the necessity for fire alarms on every level of the building. If possible, get hard-wired ones that run on electricity with a battery backup, rather than relying solely on batteries. This way, you never need to worry about them running out of power while guests are staying.

Carbon monoxide alarms are equally important, but not every house is equipped with them. Get one for each floor and especially near every sleeping area so the alarms can be heard in all rooms. Plug-in models are adequate as carbon monoxide does not rise to the ceiling but rather dissipates throughout the entire room, so standard outlets can be used.

You also want to provide a few first aid kits to place in the bathrooms and kitchen. Also, provide a fire extinguisher on every floor and in the kitchen, too. Make sure your guests are aware of the locations of these items so they can locate them easily in case of an emergency.

If your Airbnb is a shared space with more than one party of guests, locks for the bedroom doors are essential. Since keys sometimes go missing, the new lock sets that allow you to re-key the lock yourself are a great investment and provide an added layer of security for your guests.

For the front door, a keypad lock is another good investment. You can change the passcode between every guest for added security and there's no need to leave keys somewhere for guests to pick up.

Finally, you should consider installing security cameras, like the Ring Doorbell and Ring Floodlight in the front of your property. That way, you will have the camera footage if you run into a situation where a guest breaks one of your rules. You are required to disclose any surveillance devices on the property, and they are strictly forbidden in bedrooms and bathrooms.

Another good safety practice is to become friendly with your neighbors so they can keep an eye on your property and call you if they see anything suspicious.

Style and Décor

Now that you have the essentials taken care of, you can start to have some fun creating a welcoming space for your guests.

For inspiration on how to set up and stage your property, browsing through Airbnb listings to see what others have done can help. Or you can take your search to social media sites such as Pinterest and Instagram.

While browsing Pinterest, search terms like "Airbnb decorating", and you'll get thousands of results for everything from Best Airbnb Bedding to Cheap Upgrades for Your Airbnb.

On Instagram, many hosts use the platform to showcase the best features of their rental properties. Looking at their posts is a good way for you to get a feel for what is trendy in the Airbnb world.

Start with a hashtag like #airbnbhosts and prepare to be inundated with posts from all around the world with lots of ideas on how to choose and execute a style for your own property.

Choosing a Style

If you don't have a style set to guide your decisions, you could end up with confusing clutter rather than unified décor. Therefore, it is important to choose a cohesive style or two to decorate your space.

For example, modern farmhouse is a popular trend, especially in a rural setting. Clean, bright colors and lots of white with vintage-looking furniture and accessories will pull this look together.

In a city condominium, however, that would look out of place. Instead, a sleek, minimalist interior will work better.

Are you decorating a small house in an urban area or a studio apartment in an older building? Consider boho chic, with lots of bright colors and funky touches.

Of course, in a seaside cottage, you can never go wrong with the beach house look.

Whichever style you choose to set up your space with, make sure it is consistent and make sure you don't mix more than two styles together.

Painting

Even if everything is clean, an older paint job can seem dingy. Covering the walls in a fresh coat will brighten things up. Just make sure there's a flow from room to room without any jarring contrasts.

As you scroll through Instagram, you will see a lot of white walls but also some colorful exceptions. You might choose to keep the common rooms white and add color in the bedrooms or vice-versa. Adding some different hues into your house can warm up the space and give it a distinctive look that may make it stand out from the rest.

For instance, I recently had a guest on a business trip whose wife told him they have to come back together because the property has a purple room, and she loves purple.

I suggest you hire a painting crew to take care of this job. They will get it done much more quickly than you could working on your own. That way, you can shave days off your set-up schedule.

Furniture and Staging

You have a limited amount of time and a limited budget to furnish your Airbnb. Planning ahead will help make the process run smoothly.

While you are waiting to take possession of your property, you can start ordering furniture and appliances to be delivered after closing on the property. My favorite places to shop for furniture are Costco, Crate & Barrel or West Elm. You can also check out second-hand stores for some cool vintage pieces if it fits the style of your space.

Another thing to note is that while Ikea is great for some items (they sell decorative accessories, for instance), some furniture items are a nuisance to put together and can take up valuable time. It's up to you to choose whether you have enough time to assemble furniture or not.

Go through each room and make a list of the things you know you need to buy to shop more efficiently.

Let's Start with the Bedrooms
Obviously, you need beds. Beds are items you really don't want to skimp on. A bad night's sleep on an uncomfortable mattress will no doubt be reflected in reviews.

Buy new and buy good quality. There are lots of good options available for mattresses in a box with brands such as Allswell, Casper, and Tuft & Needle. These mattresses are memory foam mattresses rolled-up and delivered right to your door. Personally, I can't sleep on a memory foam mattress, so I stay away from these and think splurging on a higher-end mattress is worth its weight in reviews.

Aim for king- or queen-sized beds for your bedrooms. If possible, you should have at least one king-sized bed in one of the main bedrooms. Queen-sized mattresses work for the other bedrooms. However, you can always opt for a twin-sized bed if you are planning on hosting families with children or friends sharing a room.

You will also want to have two bedside tables in each room. People need a place to put their glass of water and cellphone, after all.

Dressers are not an absolute necessity if the closets have some shelves for those items that would otherwise go in drawers. However, a dresser can be a great statement piece in a bedroom. So if you do decide to get one, spend a little extra there and get something that will stand the test of time and constant use. Also, don't forget a mirror to hang above it.

Finally, some guests may need to do some work during their stay, so find a spot for a desk or a narrow table that can accommodate a laptop. You will also need a chair to go with it.

Moving to The Living Room

Living rooms need to be comfortable with a variety of different seating options. The anchor of the space is going to be a sofa. Or maybe two?

Depending on the size of the room and the look you are going for, two sofas facing each other can create a comfortable seating arrangement. They don't have to be identical but should be similar in size, color, and style.

Here's another place you want to spend some money to ensure pieces are in good shape and durable. Sofa beds are also a good option because you will be able to increase the number of guests who can be accommodated. Just like the beds in the bedrooms, make sure it's not going to make for a bad night's sleep.

Even though leather may seem like an easy way to create a luxurious look, all it will take is one tear or scratch and your gorgeous statement piece is in trouble. It's better to get a couch with removable cloth slipcovers. That way, if guests spill red wine or coffee on it, the covers can be switched out with a spare set while they are being cleaned.

To finish off the space, add a couple of comfortable chairs, an end table or two, and a coffee table. Again, don't go for matchy-matchy. Work within the same color and style to create a cohesive look that reflects your overall theme.

Mount a television on a wall where it can be seen by everyone. That way, you don't need a media console and can keep the space as uncluttered as possible.

Adding a gas or electric fireplace is a good way to add a cozy feel in a living room so consider that if there's room in your budget.

Onto The Dining Area

The size of the dining table and the number of chairs you select should be based on the maximum number of people who may be staying at your Airbnb. If you have three bedrooms, for instance, you will need a table to seat six.

Your table needs to be sturdy and able to withstand the wear and tear of daily use. At the same time, you definitely want it to look good. Invest your money in an attractive table that can easily be wiped clean after every meal.

When buying dining chairs, you need to bear in mind that you will have some larger guests who will need to be accommodated with sturdy seating. For that reason, stay away from delicate cane chairs or antiques.

Look for chairs rated to at least 300 pounds. This rating should accommodate most people who stay at your STR. Alternatively, use different chairs with a higher weight rating at the ends of the dining table.

Now, Let's Head Outdoors

If there is an area outdoors such as a balcony or backyard patio, invest in some comfortable seating as well as an outdoor dining table. Do not settle for the cheapest plastic chairs out there, as they will be neither comfortable nor durable.

Instead, spend your money on some mid-range wooden or metal chairs, or lounges with cushions upholstered in weatherproof materials.

What About Dressing Up the Space?

Once you select the main furniture pieces, there are other accent items you will need to consider purchasing.

If your space needs a rug, I heartily recommend machine-washable rugs like Ruggables. Ruggables are available in a huge range of colors and styles and if something spills, you can simply throw it in the washing machine. This is much better than having to take a rug in for professional cleaning or renting a rug cleaner.

You will also need to dress the windows. Keep curtains simple and make sure these are also machine-washable, too. Sites like Wayfair have thousands of colors and styles to choose from.

Each room should have both ceiling lights and accent lights. I suggest using the same ones throughout the space for a cohesive look. While you want to avoid cheap ones, don't buy really expensive ones, either. Find a mid-range line with both flush-mount and pendant lights in the same style.

Accent lamps can be more individualized. Make sure at least a few of them are good for reading.

Other Essentials

You will also need to stock the house with essentials like bedding, cookware, and dinnerware.

Let's Start with Bedding
You will need to stock up on sheets, bed coverings and pillows. One set for each bed will not be enough - two sets per bed is the bare minimum and three is recommended. You will need to purchase multiple sets for a few reasons. For one, you can save on cleaning time by changing out sheets in between guests while you clean the used ones. You should also expect to have to replace them at least once a year and obviously sooner if there are tears or stains that won't bleach out.

While you do want ones that will be comfortable and durable, you will be replacing these occasionally, so don't break the bank on deluxe sheets. Target or, even, Wal-Mart have decent sheet sets at reasonable prices. You may be surprised to know I've purchased sets from Wal-Mart, myself, that were 100% cotton with a 400-thread count for less than $30. It's amazing what you can find when you shop around! Just make sure you choose sets that are pure white because they are preferred by most guests since it's easy to see how clean they are.

Also, don't forget mattress protectors. I couldn't believe it when friends who have operated an Airbnb for years asked if I used them. Coincidentally, they were one of my first purchases.

It turns out, my friends found out how important they are the hard way: *after* their mattress was damaged. The lesson they learned was that it is essential to find a mattress protector that is not only waterproof, but pest-proof, too.

When you are buying your mattress covers, avoid cheap, plastic ones that will be noisy and uncomfortable. Instead, focus your search on a quality mattress cover that zips on, fits tight and is soft to the touch. Amazon has some great options.

When it comes to a comforter, don't just buy an individual comforter, go for a set. Sets with matching shams will give you a more finished look. Plus, with two pillows in crisp white pillowcases and two in shams, your bed will look picture-perfect.

For comforter sets, you want something that will be lightweight but warm and easy to clean. Again, Amazon has some great basic bedding sets in a variety of colors. You should have two sets for each bed so there is a spare on hand.

Pick up a few throws along the way, as well. They'll come in handy not just in the bedrooms, but also in the living room. Neutral colors that will coordinate with all your rooms will work best.

You can also get pillows at Wal-Mart that are very comfortable and well within budget. Get four pillows for a queen or king bed. You want to make sure you buy the correct size to match the bed, as standard-size pillows on a king bed will look cheap. Don't forget to buy pillow protectors, too.

Moving On to The Bathroom

Of course, the bathroom will need to be stocked with towels and washcloths. Plan on purchasing at least two per guest. Depending on the space, I like to set towels in the bathroom for a spa-like feel, but I've also placed them in the bedroom, too.

Same as the sheets, stick to all white towels. You can pick up some towels at Costco or, once again, Wal-Mart has reasonably priced 100% cotton ones that are a decent size.

You'll also need bathmats and shower curtains. Keep the bathmats a neutral color. With the shower curtain, choosing ones with a pattern is a good way to inject some personality into what can otherwise be a characterless space. Make sure these items are easy to wash and dry, but also have some extras on hand to speed up the between-bookings setup.

Finally, if you have a laundry room as one of your amenities, invest in a good washer and dryer set. You will want to include an ironing board and iron, too.

Now to The Dining Area

For dining, you should have at least two of everything for the maximum number of people your Airbnb can accommodate. Consider how you stock your own home. I'm sure you have more than one plate and bowl per person living with you.

At a minimum, supply two of each of the following per guest:

- dinner plates

- salad plates

- bowls

- mugs

- drinking glasses

- wine glasses

- silverware

In addition, you will need at least a couple of serving bowls and utensils. You will want to purchase extras of these, too, so you will have a replacement if something breaks. While some hosts recommend buying the Corelle brand because their pieces are indestructible, I feel they just come across as cheap. I prefer ceramic ones because they are sturdier and you can find some at a good price. Stick with white since it is the most versatile and check Ikea, Target, or Costco for inexpensive, durable options that look good.

While cloth napkins may seem like a wise choice both for cost and the environment, you would need a lot to stock your Airbnb for a week for six guests. You're better off buying paper ones in bulk at Costco.

Finally, Let's Finish with The Kitchen

A well-equipped kitchen is going to make your guests very happy. That's what you want, right?

Starting with appliances, at a minimum, you need a stove and refrigerator. A dishwasher is highly recommended because no one wants to waste time washing dishes on vacation.

Of course, you need a microwave. Avoid built-in microwaves because it is harder to swap out than a countertop model if it does break. You will also need a toaster. Instead of a pop-up toaster buy a toaster oven/air fryer combo that can be used for a variety of cooking tasks.

Coffee makers and blenders are other essential kitchen appliances. Buy a Keurig or similar coffee maker for ease of use. Then, make sure you buy a blender that is strong enough for chopping ice, in case guests want to make a pitcher of Margaritas. You don't need to provide a stand mixer, but a hand-held electric mixer is an inexpensive option.

While I love my cast-iron pans for my home kitchen, I wouldn't stock an Airbnb with them as they require too much maintenance. Instead, I recommend a set of different sized non-stick pots and pans. Add a couple of casserole dishes and sheet pans for the oven, and a kettle to boil water on the stove. You also want to have a pair of oven mitts on hand, too.

Then, choose a set of stainless-steel nesting bowls that can be used for food preparation and serving. If you buy a glass set with lids, they can also be used to store leftovers in the fridge.

Essential cooking utensils include:

- measuring cups

- measuring spoons

- cooking spoons (either metal or wood)

- soup ladle

- spatulas

- tongs

- grater

- peeler

- scissors

- whisk

- pizza cutter

- can opener

- grill tools (if you have a barbecue grill)

You can usually find sets that include most or all these items together.

High-quality knives should also be purchased. At a bare minimum, you need a chef knife, a serrated knife, and a few steak knives. Buy a set that comes in a knife block to help keep them sharp.

Finally, make it easy for your guests to clean up after themselves by purchasing a supply of kitchen towels, and a broom and dustpan. Rubber gloves are a good idea, too. You can buy all of these at Target, Costco, or Wal-Mart.

While you don't need to buy top of the line items, don't buy the cheapest either, so items won't have to be replaced as often.

Consumables
Consumable goods are things that get used up on a regular basis and you will need lots of those in your Airbnb.

In the bathroom, of course you must supply toilet paper. You really can't go wrong with Costco. They have big packages that will last a long time.

While your guests may arrive with their preferred toiletries, it is a good idea to have some basics on hand in case they forget or run out. Don't feel like you have to go the hotel route with individual packages of soaps and shampoos. I have found that regular size bottles of shampoo, conditioner and body washes have been used without complaint from my guests. I like to get unscented ones in case guests have allergies, but also provide scented options, too.

At the sink, I have pump bottles of soap and hand sanitizer. I also have a basket with items such as disposable shower caps, disposable razors, feminine hygiene products, a sewing kit, a hot water bottle, and a first aid kit in case of a middle of the night emergency, or a guest forgets something.

The kitchen is another place where things will need to be restocked, regularly. The basic food supplies like oil, basic seasonings, and coffee and tea won't spoil. But, you or your cleaning crew will need to monitor them to see if you need refills. While these essential items are really all that's necessary, you can choose to go beyond that and stock the refrigerator with basic condiments and bottled water, too.

Other items that are appreciated are a roll each of plastic wrap, aluminum foil and plenty of paper towels. Cleaning supplies including dishwashing detergent, dishwasher pods and an all-purpose antibacterial cleaning spray, are a must.

In your laundry room, stock unscented laundry detergent and dryer sheets. Again, it is best to purchase most of these items in bulk at Costco.

Finishing Touches

I saved this for last, but that doesn't mean it is not important. Accessories and artwork will make your Airbnb stand out in the listings. Without them, you will have a characterless space that will not reach out and grab guests' attention as a great place to visit. I know when guests send booking requests to me, they often mention the décor is part of the appeal.

"Important" does not have to mean "expensive"! In fact, let's start with *free*. When I set up my first Airbnb, I was able to pull a lot of decorative items out of storage and use them to stage my property.

This included framed pictures I didn't have room for in my own home as well as assorted vases and decorative pieces. I even used some of my dad's old paint-by-number paintings. These are actually quite trendy now and add a real vintage charm to the space. However, don't use pieces that are of sentimental value that you wouldn't want to lose through damage or theft.

Once you've exhausted your own resources, check out Facebook Marketplace online or visit some second-hand stores. Your goal is to find interesting, attractive pieces to add character to your space.

It's also always fun to include items that relate to the location of your Airbnb. For instance, if you are setting up a lakeside cabin, vintage finds like an oar to mount on a wall or lean in a corner are perfect. In a city condominium, framed historic photographs of local landmarks or old maps are an interesting touch.

Finally, stores like Target, Costco, Amazon, and Wal-Mart can help you fill in the last empty spots. Ikea, as I mentioned, has great options for tiny décor and small plants. Avoid anything that looks like it should be hanging in a hotel bedroom. After all, your guests chose not to stay in one of those.

Try to have some fun with this last stage of setting up your Airbnb. If you enjoy what you see, odds are good that your guests will too. However, don't get carried away and fill up the entire space with accent pieces. The last thing you want is a cluttered look.

This is the point in the decorating process where you may want to hire a home stager for a day or so to help you make your property truly photo ready. Stagers are pros at using what you have and showing it off to its best advantage. They've been setting up homes to sell for a few decades now and their skills are perfectly suited to helping you sell your Airbnb to guests.

However, if you have a flair for decorating yourself, go ahead and trust your own instincts.

Action Items to DO NOW!:

1. Define the Experience You Want to Create for Your Guests
Drawing off your research into other properties and considering the location and features of your property, make a plan for how to create an enjoyable experience for your guests.

2. Determine What Amenities You Can Offer Your Guests
List the unique amenities your property already has as well as amenities you would like to provide. Then see how they stack up against your competition and your budget.

3. Choose A Cleaning Service
Interview at least three different cleaners or cleaning services to have one ready for your first booking.

4. Purchase Security Features
Be ready to equip your place with security cameras (like the Ring Doorbell and Ring Floodlight outside your place), door locks, smoke alarms, and CO_2 detectors when you take possession.

5. Choose Your Style and Start Decorating
Know how much money you have to spend to furnish your space. Stay within those limits as you purchase all the essential items for your property. If it comes down to

it, make a "must buy" list and a "buy later" list to delay low-priority items for later when you have more cash.

6. Set up Your Property and Stage it

As soon as you take possession, get your property painted and furnished with everything needed for your guests' comfort and convenience.

Chapter Five

Listing Your Property on Airbnb

Your Airbnb listing is an opportunity to showcase your property to potential guests and to describe why they will love staying at your place.

Obviously, the essentials of location, rooms and amenities matter very much. But, if that's all you have to offer, people looking for more will go elsewhere to find it. That's why you need a "wow" factor to attract them, such as stunning photos and compelling content to draw them in and encourage them to book with you.

For an apartment, condo, house, or unique stay, you will only need one listing. However, if you are renting multiple rooms separately for one property, you need to create a different listing for each room.

Before you plunge in and start working on your listing, remember a couple of things. Airbnb will walk you through the process one step at a time. If you feel overwhelmed or need additional guidance, you can also reference this book at any time.

Also, don't worry if you miss anything. Even after your listing goes live, you can always go back at any time and make it better. Plus, once you have some experience hosting, you will want to go back in and improve it by highlighting things your guests say they love about your Airbnb.

Let's get started.

Have Professional Photos Taken

Obviously, you need to wait until your property is camera-ready to have pictures taken. Line up a professional photographer to make sure they are available once you are ready for photos.

You may think photos from your cellphone will be good enough. They won't be! Professional photographers have the skills and equipment to make your Airbnb look its best. Spending the money on a pro will pay off in increased bookings.

Use the same process as finding a cleaner – interview at least three photographers and choose the one you like the best. One word of caution: I've heard from other hosts that they were not happy with their experience working with photographers supplied by Airbnb. Find a professional photographer on your own by asking for recommendations from other hosts or doing a Google search for "Airbnb photographers" in your area.

When you find a photographer, you will be ready to schedule an appointment as soon as possible once your staging is complete. Make sure you schedule them during the "Golden Hour" because it will make a difference in the quality of your photos by giving them a warmer, softer glow. This is when the sun is lower in the sky during the early morning or late afternoon/early evening. Keep in mind your photos should be sized to at least 1024 x 683px resolution and a width to length aspect ratio of 3:2.

When your photographer is at your property, tell them you want to make sure guests will be able to "experience" your property without actually having been there before. Have them take several shots so you have plenty to choose from.

Instruct them to take photos from different angles as they go through each room. Then, have them snap a few shots of the outdoor areas so guests will get a good sense of the surroundings. Also, make sure you grab a few photos of yourself and your family enjoying the property.

Finally, don't limit your photos to ones from your own property. Another great photo opportunity is to take shots of nearby points of interest and places guests can entertain themselves while staying there.

Listing Your Property

About Your Place

The first question you will be asked is "Which of these best describes your place?". Airbnb shows you a list of options that include the different types of properties. For example, you have familiar house, apartment, cabin or guesthouse. You also have the unique stays like a container, earth home, houseboat or castle.

Once you've made your selection, you are taken to the next question: "What type of place will your guests have?". The options are "an entire place, a private room or a shared room".

Next, you are taken to the section where you will enter the address of your property. Once your address is entered, you will see a pin drop of the general area on the map. The address is only shared with guests after they book with you.

You have the choice to keep the pin drop at a general location or you can click the toggle button to show your specific location. If you click the toggle button, it will not show your exact location, it will zoom in on the pin drop. The next page asks you if the pin is in the correct location.

Once you confirm, you are moved to the next page that asks you to "share some basics about your place". This means, describe how many guests you can host, how many bedrooms, beds, and bathrooms there are.

Amenities

You don't need to physically go through your Airbnb to make a list of amenities you have to offer. In this section, Airbnb provides suggestions for you to simply click and choose the ones available at your property. Pay attention to the safety items listed. You should have all four: smoke alarms, first aid kit, carbon monoxide detector and fire extinguisher.

Remember to take note of the amenities you do have at your property but are not listed here. You will have the opportunity to add them in a separate section after you go through the initial setup.

Keep in mind Airbnb adds new amenities, regularly. It's worth scrolling through every now and then to see if there is something new since you initially set up your listing.

Photos

If you are wondering how many photos you should add to your listing, the short answer is "lots". Airbnb's upper limit is 100, so don't be afraid to use as many photos as needed to showcase your property. At first, you will start with your first five photos.

When guests start searching for properties to book, they will see one photo for your listing, along with many other properties jostling for attention. This is where you advertise the absolute best feature of your property to make it stand out from the rest.

Obviously, you want to put your best photo here to get them to click on the thumbnail and explore further. Airbnb calls this photo, the Hero Photo.

For instance, in a high-rise condominium, it could be the view out the window to an iconic skyline, while a rustic cabin might feature a cozy living room with a fire blazing in the fireplace.

Once you've chosen the Hero Photo, it's time to select the next four most important photos.

On your computer, go to current listings on Airbnb. Click on any of the thumbnails and you will see one large photo on the left – the Hero Photo - with four more arranged in a grid on the right. These five photos need to be compelling enough to make visitors want to explore further. All the persuasive text in the world won't have the same impact as these five pictures.

Depending on what you choose for the Hero Photo, those next four photos should be selected from the best photos of the kitchen, living room, master bedroom, bathroom, or an outdoor shot. Not sure if they have enough impact? It doesn't hurt to ask a friend to look them over and get a second opinion when you're finished.

Once you have the top five taken care of, you can continue adding more now, or you can add them later. It's important to pay attention to the order in which they will appear in your listing.

You may be tempted to arrange them by room to "walk" the guest through the house: five of the kitchen, followed by five of the bathroom, etc. Resist this urge. You don't want someone browsing through to lose interest before they even see most of the property.

Instead, take the best shot of each of the rooms or spaces and put them at the top (after the first five, obviously). Then, you can go back and arrange the rest by room. It's sort of like a newspaper article, where the first paragraph covers all the essential facts and then adds more detail further on.

You may think one photo of each room, along with a couple of the outdoor areas, would be enough. However, I recommend using three to five pictures of every room in the property showcasing the different angles. This includes the bedrooms, living and dining spaces, the kitchen and even hallways. Then, add at least that many photos of the exterior of the house, including a clear shot of the front so guests will easily recognize it when they arrive.

Does your property have a great view? What about outdoor amenities such as a hot tub, deck, firepit, or pool? Add several shots of each feature.

Remember, you're not only showing people what your property looks like, but how it can be enjoyed. Think of how effective a picture of a lit firepit with a couple of comfortable chairs and a table set with wine and a charcuterie board would be.

One note about firepits: if you're offering this as an amenity, do you provide firewood? Taking a photo of this lets guests know they don't have to bring their own.

There are several other images you can add to help guests decide whether to choose your place to stay. If you have impressively fast Wi-Fi, take a screenshot of a speed test. Draw up a floorplan of the house using a site like Floorplanner.com where you can make it 3-dimensional if you want.

Obviously, you won't choose every picture from the photo shoot. Choose the best you have. You can probably see you're looking at around 25 to 30 photos for a one-bedroom apartment. By that number, a 3-bedroom house should have around 50.

A few things to note about arranging your photos. The squares can be arranged by dragging and dropping them to a new square. Airbnb also asks you if you want to try putting your best photos first. If you click "Try it", it will arrange your photos for you. I don't recommend this because only you know your property best and its greatest features.

Also, when you click on the three dots in the corner of each photo, you have the opportunity to edit the photos (which isn't necessary because you have professional photos) and add a caption up to 250 characters. You don't have to use up all the characters, here. Use as many as you need to promote your property as the ideal place stay.

Remember, anyone checking out your listing is going to look at the photos before reading any of your content. This may be your only chance to emphasize the amenities you have to offer before they move on to the next listing.

Get creative and describe the experiences they could enjoy in your Airbnb. Is it a picture of a clawfoot bathtub? Try something like: "Unwind and take a moment to relax in this gorgeous tub after a long day hiking."

When you start adding captions, make sure you write one for every single photo. Otherwise, your listing will look unfinished. Once you have been hosting for a while, go through your reviews and find some quotes that describe how actual guests enjoyed their experience. This will make it very easy for prospective guests to put themselves into the picture.

Creating a Name and Title

First, you want to name your Airbnb. Think of the name as your property's "brand" and come up with something creative, yet descriptive. It can be related to the theme of your property or the location it's in. It can also focus on a unique aspect of your property or a point of interest nearby. Keep in mind, the name is a good way to make your listing stand out from the rest.

For inspiration, go to Airbnb and start looking at other properties. I just clicked on a few and found "Cast-Away Lodge", "The Eagle's Nest" and "Midnight Manor", among many others.

The name of your property is not the same as the title of your listing. The title, which is the next section, is your first chance to catch the interest of your potential guests and should be a brief 32-character introduction to your listing.

You want to use as many, if not ALL 32 characters you have available to you, to showcase the most important selling points for your property. It can include location, number of rooms and one special amenity that makes it stand out from the rest.

If you're in a location that attracts business travelers, for instance, you might want to highlight your fast Wi-Fi. In a city where visitors will be heading out to see the sights, being close to the subway might attract them. In a vacation spot, a pool table or movie theatre could be a deciding factor as a potential guest scrolls through listings.

You might have to use some abbreviations to fit everything you want into 32 characters. For instance, "BR" instead of "bedroom" will work.

Finally, your title is not carved in stone. You can change it seasonally as local attractions change. Once it's too cold for visits to the beach in a northern resort town, for instance, you could change your title to highlight local skiing slopes, instead.

Description

The description for your property is next and is limited to 500 characters. It is best practice to start with an attention-grabbing statement that will quickly interest prospective guests about your property. If you don't know where to start when writing your description, Airbnb provides a section that asks you to choose two "highlights" from a clickable list. It is not mandatory for you choose two highlights. However, if you do choose two, you will see on the next screen there will be a prewritten introduction to your description using the words you chose.

For the rest of the characters, highlight the **most** attractive amenities your Airbnb offers. You can expand with more details when you complete the initial setup. First, talk briefly about your property (1-2 sentences), its benefits and key amenities. The goal is to make your guests want to click the "see more" link so they can review all the other features in detail.

You don't need to list the details of how many bedrooms or bathrooms there are as those are found elsewhere.

Then, create a picture with words of what the experience of staying at your Airbnb will be like. Describe for them the vibe both indoors and outside. Is it a rustic country cabin surrounded by forest and lake? Or a sleek city loft a few steps from a vibrant nightlife scene?

Use up your 500 characters and keep in mind spelling errors will be flagged for you, but grammar will not.

Make sure you proof-read your description and then get someone else to proofread it after.

Completing Your Listing

The next section asks you who you want to welcome for your first reservation: any Airbnb guest or an experienced guest. They allow you to choose who will book your first reservation and after the first booking anyone will be able to book.

What's the difference? If you choose "Any Airbnb guest", your listing will be available to everyone on the Airbnb platform. This means your listing will be exposed to more people and you may get your first booking faster. An "experienced guest" is someone who has stayed at a minimum of three other Airbnb's before, their identity has been verified, their payment information is already confirmed and they have a history of complying with Airbnb policies.

In my opinion, you are in this to start a successful business. You should feel confident in the research and work you put into your Airbnb so it shouldn't matter whether you have an experienced guest or not. However, an experienced guest may be able to give you better insight as they have stayed at other properties before. Choose the option you feel most comfortable with.

Dynamically Set Your Pricing

The next step is to enter your nightly rate. This is the rate you will earn per night. Guests will see a price with Airbnb fees added on. You should have done your research with AirDNA or other similar programs and by checking out your competition.

Here, Airbnb recommends offering a 20% discount to help your listing stand out and encourage your first three guests to book. As a new host, this is a good strategy to implement. A lower nightly rate will encourage guests to take a chance on a listing with no reviews.

The important thing to keep in mind is you should not have a set price for one night and keep it the same. You should change it up once in a while. Consider gas prices, for instance. Gas prices fluctuate based on supply and demand. This is why they always seem to rise right before a holiday weekend - more people will be driving and buying gas creating a higher demand, so prices rise.

Similarly, there will be periods when more people are looking to book an Airbnb and other times when demand in your area is down. It's not the same across the country, obviously. For instance, a Cape Cod STR is much more likely to be fully booked in summer, while a Miami condo or an Aspen chalet will get the most bookings in winter.

If you don't change your rates to reflect the fluctuations in demand, you're going to have two issues. First, when Airbnbs in your area are busy, you will be missing out on potential profits if your prices are too low. You may be fully booked, but you could have made more money because there's nowhere else available to stay.

Second, in your slow season, if your prices are too high, potential guests will have lots of cheaper options to choose from close by.

What are you to do? Dynamically price your listing!

Dynamic pricing is a pricing strategy where you adjust your rates to reflect supply and demand.

Airbnb may give you suggestions on what to charge, but it's not very helpful. You can easily see from checking out local listings that other hosts are charging well above Airbnb's suggested pricing for similar properties. If you follow their recommendations, it's likely you will lose money.

Instead, you can allow sites such as PriceLabs, Wheelhouse, or Beyond (formerly Beyond Pricing) to automate the dynamic pricing for you. There is a monthly fee associated with these platforms. For example, PriceLabs charges hosts a monthly fee per listing. Feedback from most hosts is the time these services save you is worth it. Especially when you have more than one property.

These sites use their algorithms to monitor a variety of different factors and will automatically adjust your rates for you. For instance, they gather all the information about local events that will increase visits to your area and raise rates accordingly on those dates.

They can also adjust your rates according to when guests book. For instance, guests booking a couple of months out can be charged a lower rate than guests booking at the last minute. Plus, if you have some awkward gaps of a day or two in your calendar, they will reduce rates close to the date to get those days booked.

Security Disclosures

In the last section, Airbnb asks you about the security of your property. This is where you will need to disclose if there are any security cameras and their exact location or any potential dangers on the property such as weapons or dangerous animals.

Reviewing Your Listing

Here is where you make sure everything looks good enough to publish. You can do this now, or you can choose to publish and do it later. If you do choose to publish, you will have to click on "confirm important details", first. Click "start" and you will be taken to confirm your phone number and identity. Once you finish, click "Publish Listing". Guests will be able to start booking with you after 24 hours, giving you enough time to finish more listing details not included in the initial setup.

Further down on the main page, in the section titled "Your next steps", there are other boxes that show you what is left to do.

Instant Book

One of the first things you should look at is Instant Book. I was advised not to use it for the first few bookings when I opened my first Airbnb.

It's all in the name - instead of going through the process of making a reservation request, guests can automatically book your STR if they meet your requirements.

Not surprisingly, guests like the Instant Book option and it's one of the filters they can use to narrow their search. If you have Instant Book turned on, you will appear in more searches and probably get more bookings. Even if they don't filter for it, Airbnb's algorithm automatically puts Instant Book properties above the rest in search results.

Interesting story about Instant Bookings, a host friend of mine came home to find a guest sitting on their front porch waiting to be let in because they didn't see the notification on their phone. Luckily, Airbnb allows you to build in safeguards to prevent surprises like this.

You can restrict Instant Bookings to whatever number of days before check-in makes you most comfortable and you can cancel Instant Book reservations penalty-free.

Click on the "Instant Book options" box to review the settings. When you click on the box, it will take you to a page where you can toggle Instant Book on or off. When it is turned on, there is an additional toggle button for you to choose whether or not to only allow guests who have followed Airbnb policies and have good reviews.

In the end, it's a personal decision you need to make for yourself, but if you want to maximize your bookings, it's worth considering.

As I was advised, I suggest leaving it off for your first few bookings until you understand more about how things work within the platform and turn it on once you've manually reviewed a few bookings. Then, you can decide if using Instant Book is right for you.

Calendar

Start setting up your calendar, next. Here you have the option of setting minimum and maximum trip lengths. I like to set a minimum of two nights to keep people who want a place to "party" for a night from booking with me. For a maximum stay, I set it to 365 nights because I don't live there and don't want to place limits on how long someone wants to stay.

Then, you can select how far into the future someone can book and how much time you need between bookings. Choose how far in advance you want your calendar shown to potential guests. The drop-down menu gives you the option to choose from no availability, three, six, nine, 12 months or all dates. For the in between bookings time, plan accordingly to how long you need to clean and prepare the property for the next guests. These dates will automatically be blocked off on your calendar.

The final section here takes you to your calendar to customize certain dates. In the calendar view, you can choose to view your calendar by the month or by year. You probably want the year view, as it's easier to navigate.

Here, you can block off any dates you don't want to be available. For instance, if you have an Airbnb in Cape Cod and are planning to use it yourself for a couple of weeks in August, simply select those dates and click the "x".

Finally, you can also add custom settings for dates you select. With dates selected, you can adjust the pricing, length of stays and discounts for those specific dates only.

For instance, you may want to limit stays in peak season to at least a week or apply out-of-season discounts to increase your chances of getting booked when things slow down. Create as many custom settings that will work for you.

Once you start getting bookings, they will automatically show up on your calendar and anyone searching for an Airbnb on those dates will not see your property in their search results.

You can always go into your calendar at the top of the main page to fine-tune your availability. Confirm the calendar settings and move to the next box on the home page.

Cancellation Policy

Here is where you establish your cancellation policy for a stay less than 28 nights and stays longer than 28 days. You get to choose how flexible or strict you want to be on this. Since guests do change their mind and cancel bookings, you don't want to be left with an empty property when you could have been making money.

You decide how soon before their arrival date guests can cancel without penalty. That could be as close as one day before arrival to as long as 30 days before.

Balance the need for income security against the risk of scaring off potential guests and choose what works for you. Confirm your settings and move onto the next section.

House Rules

The next box is where you will set up check-in and check-out times, the number of guests you can accommodate, and the house rules your guests will need to follow. You can check whether or not you allow pets, smoking, events, or filming.

With check-in and check-out times, find a nice balance that will make your guests happy and not leave your cleaning crew feeling rushed. Having too early a check-out time will discourage bookings because no one wants to be rushed in the morning. On the other hand, don't make it too late as it will make it challenging to prepare the property for the next booking.

Along with choosing check-in and check-out times, you can set "quiet hours" for when guests must keep noise levels down. You can also adjust the number of guests you can accommodate before adding additional rules.

When it comes to house rules, start with the basics. Then, provide any additional rules you may have such as whether you allow shoes to be worn in the house or if candles are permitted on the premises.

Maintain a certain level of balance when you create additional rules for your Airbnb. You don't want to have too many rules because it can make you seem difficult and leave your guests with a poor experience. On the other hand, these rules are necessary to protect your property and your business.

Remember, you want your guests to have the best experience possible at your Airbnb. Limit your rules to the essentials, make them reasonable, and communicate them clearly in a friendly manner.

Obviously, you're not going to be hanging around to make sure all the rules are followed. Your cleaners will be able to tell you if there is evidence of a rule not being followed. Or, if you are friendly with your neighbors, they can also tell you if certain rules are being broken. Like, if your guest has a late-night party.

After some time hosting you can always update the rules based on your experience of knowing what *can* go wrong. You want to make sure the rules are always up to date so there are no unpleasant surprises for guests when they arrive.

Promotions
The last box allows you to review your weekly (7-27 nights) or monthly (28 nights or more) promotions. These promotions are discounts you offer to encourage longer stays. More discounts such as early-bird or

last-minute discounts can be found under the "Pricing and Availability" section we will discuss in a moment.

Other Settings to Adjust

You went through Airbnb prompts to set up your listing. However, there are still important parts of your listing to complete, fully, before you take it live. From the main page, navigate to Menu > Listing. Click on the name of your property.

Under "Listing Details" you can scroll down through the various sections available to update. Go through each section and update missing information. Here are a few to pay attention to:

Listing Basics

The first thing you can update is the listing title. Previously, Airbnb gave you 32 characters. Now, you will find there are 50. The reason they had you enter 32 characters at first is because that is all a guest can see on their phone. Add as many more characters as you would like to get as close to 50 as possible.

Remember when I told you, you would be able to expand on the description after you go through the initial setup? This is where you have the chance. When you click to edit "listing description", you will see three new options below the "description" box without character limits.

The first box is "the space". This is where you expand on room and outdoor details to draw attention to your Airbnb's amenities and "sell" your listing to potential guests. It's a good place to highlight amenities like available streaming services, fast Wi-Fi speed, or special appliances, like an air fryer.

Be as descriptive as possible to create an accurate picture so the reader can envision exactly what the property is like. Also, make it easier to read by breaking it up into short paragraphs, rather than having a solid wall of text.

Make your words count so there is little confusion as to what your guests are getting. It's important to not oversell your property when you describe it. You do not want a guest to be disappointed by their reality because I can guarantee you will be disappointed in their review.

"Guest access" basically tells the reader what areas they can use on the property. For instance, in an apartment Airbnb, guests may be able to use a pool or gym that is available to all residents.

Under "other details to note", this is the place where you can add additional amenities you have but were not in the original checklist. For instance, if you arranged for a discount at a local boat rental or museum, this would be a good place to mention it.

Make sure you don't just list them in this section, "talk" about the additional amenities. For example, "In addition to the amenities listed, this property offers…"

You might want to circle back to this section after you go through the rest of the listing process to see what's missing that you can add here.

Another sub-section to pay attention to is "listing status". This is where you will go to activate your listing by clicking the radio button next to "Listed". If you click the radio button for "Deactivate", this will remove your property completely. Once you've deactivated your listing, you will have to recreate it over again if you change your mind.

If you prefer to unlist your property temporarily, "Unlisted" is the way to go, as it gives you the option of simply turning it back on again. This option takes you out of search results until you switch back to "Listed".

"Snoozed" is another option you can choose. However, you won't see this option until after you publish your listing. If you click on "Snoozed", you are taken to the calendar to indicate when you want your listing to be unavailable. Choose the dates you want to block off so your listing is not visible during that time.

Finally, "Deactivate" removes your property entirely.

Right about now you're probably nervous (and excited) at the thought of clicking "Listed" to take your listing live. You can do this if you want – remember you have 24 hours before it is "officially" listed - but we still have some more ground to cover.

Additional Location Details

The first section to pay attention to is "Location". Here you will see sub sections you did not see previously: "neighborhood description", "getting around", "location sharing", and "scenic views".

The "neighborhood description" is a place you can describe the general character of the area your property is located. Go into detail about specific points of interest guests can visit. Recommend some good restaurants and entertainment venues to convince them this is the place to be.

"Getting around" is where to place information about parking at your property and public transportation. Not all city properties will have free parking available, so make sure your guests are aware if they will have to pay for overnight parking and where it is accessible. Also provide tips about public transportation, if available in the area.

Under "location sharing" you can either choose a "specific location" to openly list your address for everyone to see. Or, you can show a "General Location" which only shows the area where your property is located.

To me, the latter is the safer option for everyone because you get to keep the location of your Airbnb private until you have an actual guest. In addition to only showing the address to guests that book, you can take it a step further. There is another toggle button you can choose to turn on. When the toggle is on, you can choose to release the exact location once the opportunity for the guest to cancel for free has passed.

Clicking to edit "scenic views" will bring up a checkbox so you can choose the scenic views your property has, if applicable.

The "accessibility" section is a place to show guests with mobility needs that they can feel confident staying at your property. If you don't go in and change the accessibility list, all of the items are pre-set to "No". Don't spend any time with it unless you do have a space suitable for someone with mobility issues. Unless you have a space with no stairs and 32-inch-wide doorways and no thresholds, there probably isn't a point in completing this part.

If you do have some of the features listed that will help guests who need those accommodations, scroll through the list and see what's there. This will help guests filter their search to find your property (and others) that are suitable for their needs.

Pricing and Availability

As I mentioned earlier, you can set your "early-bird" and "last-minute" stay discounts here. You can also set "length-of-stay" discounts. For example, you can set a discount for someone who books for eight or 12 weeks.

In the "additional charges" section, there are a few optional fees you can add to your base rate. You can add your cleaning fee along with pet fees, additional guest fees and your weekend pricing.

With cleaning fees, you may choose to absorb your cleaning costs into your base daily or weekly rate. Some hosts charge a separate cleaning fee which is a one-time service fee. In other words, the fee is the same whether a guest books for one night, one week, or one month.

Standard cleaning fees can vary depending on the size of the property and whether hosts do the work themselves or hire it out. Previously, cleaning and other additional fees were not included in the rate shown in the search results and many guests complained they saw the full price without knowing what it entailed, until checkout.

Now, guests have a choice of whether they would like to see one total price, or they can see an itemized list to show them the cost break-down before starting the booking process.

Personal Profile

Remember, every part of your listing is a way to persuade guests your Airbnb is the best choice for them. Your personal profile is no exception, and it is a way to introduce yourself to guests.

Head over to the top right corner of the main page and edit your profile details. Start with a good picture that is focused on your face. Then, turn your attention to the About section.

This is not a dating profile, but here is where you will provide some information about yourself. In about 50 to 100 words, give guests a sense of who you are. Your background, occupation and leisure activities are all good things to include here.

Take Your Listing Live

Remember, anything in your listing can be changed at any time. In fact, I recommend you occasionally look at your listing to see what you can improve.

If you haven't done this already, there's only one thing left to do: publish your listing. Head back to the "listing basics" section and click the radio button next to "listed".

MAKE THIS MOVE! And celebrate! At some point, you have to take the plunge and take your big step into Airbnb hosting. You're starting a new phase of your life as soon as you click "save".

Action Items to DO NOW!:

1. Have Your Property Photographed...Professionally
Once your property is staged and ready, it's time for the photo shoot. Great pictures are absolutely essential to attract guests to your Airbnb.

2. Choose Your Best 5 Photos and Arrange the Rest
Use lots of photos and arrange them strategically to drive bookings. The first five photos should be the absolute best. Don't forget that captions are a powerful tool for adding context.

3. Create a Catchy Name and Title
Create a Name for your Airbnb. In 32, and then 50 characters, fit in as many selling points as possible.

4. Create Your Property Description
Use this section to give your potential guests the details of the property. Also, give them a sense of what they can expect the experience to be like when they stay at your Airbnb.

5. Set Up Dynamic Pricing
Use a service like PriceLabs to take care of the dynamic pricing for your Airbnb.

6. Optimize Your Listing

After the initial setup, edit sections in your listing to ensure every detail is communicated.

7. Take Your Listing Live

Congratulations! Take some time to recognize and celebrate all the hard work you've accomplished so far.

CHAPTER SIX

Running a Smooth Operation

Now you have listed your Airbnb property, it's time to focus on all the elements that contribute to making it a success on an ongoing basis.

Soft Launch

Once you take your listing live, it's a good idea to block off the first week on your calendar to take your Airbnb for a test run, otherwise known as a "soft launch". Guests will be able to start booking with you after that, so use this time wisely.

The soft launch is your opportunity to experience your Airbnb property as a "guest" to see if you missed something, need to make last minute changes, or if there are any bugs in your operation that need to be worked out.

First, stay there a couple of nights, yourself. When you stay at your vacation rental as a "guest", you will be able to test everything out and remedy things that need to be updated or changed.

The next phase of your soft launch is to ask some reliable friends to stay there and give you some feedback on what needs to be tweaked before you *really* open for business. It's especially helpful if they are experienced Airbnb hosts or at least have stayed at other STR properties because they will have something to compare your place with.

Going through this process will give you more confidence in your property for when your first real guests do arrive.

Cleaning and Maintenance

Owner's Closet
In Chapter 4, I mentioned setting aside a space for an owner's or housekeeping closet. This is a locked room or closet on the property that only you and your cleaning staff will have access to. It should have everything necessary to prepare the property in between guests without having to lug in fresh linens and cleaning supplies each time.

Some hosts may use an extra linen, bathroom, or bedroom closet. The laundry room can also work for hosts who choose to keep the laundry facilities off-limits to guests.

The owner's closet is important not only to ensure smooth turnovers when you have subsequent bookings – one after the other with a short duration for cleaning in between - but also for ongoing security reasons.

For instance, this is where your Wi-Fi access and router should be kept, as well as controls for security cameras. If they aren't behind a locked door, your guests could reset the Wi-Fi and turn off the cameras.

This is also where all the items needed between bookings should be kept like extra bedding, towels, and washcloths (aside of the extras you leave out for guests). Having more linens ready to go in this locked closet means your cleaner can make the beds with fresh sheets while the dirty ones are being washed.

Other essentials to keep in this space are items like garbage bags, toilet paper, tissues, paper towels, soaps and shampoos, and dish detergent. You should also keep excess supplies of coffee and bottled water here, after setting out enough for the number of guests and length of stay.

Most of your cleaning supplies should also be kept in this closet, however, you will want to keep some out for guests to use. This closet will also be a great place to store your vacuum cleaner and even a small rug and upholstery cleaner. This way, any stains left behind by the departing guests can be quickly dealt with. You should leave a broom and dustpan, and possibly a handheld or inexpensive stick vacuum for guests to use.

While you don't want guests to be able to walk right in and take what they want, you still want it to be accessible in case an emergency arises where they need something like fresh bedsheets. For this reason, it's best to install a keyless lock system so you can send them the code and they can get in without you or your cleaner having to drive out at midnight to unlock it for them.

Creating a Cleaning Checklist

Creating a cleaning checklist helps you to establish standards to allow a consistent cleaning every turnaround while making sure nothing is missed. For your first cleaning, I recommend you clean the property yourself. You will want to take notes on how you cleaned it, so you know what to include on your checklist. A great time to make this list is the first time you clean your unit and then again during your soft launch, after you stay there. Then, you can double check your list when your friends stay at your place. Cleaning the property yourself, at first, will help you discover and set standards for what exactly needs to be done each time.

The next time you need your property cleaned, have your cleaners clean while you watch how they clean the property. This serves two purposes. One, you can see if they clean everything you did. Two, you can see how they clean to see if there's anything you can add to your notes.

When you have a turn cleaning the property and the cleaners have theirs, you can then compare notes to create the final cleaning checklist for the property. When your cleaning game plan is documented, it will be easier to train more cleaners how to clean the property in the future. It will also ensure everyone who cleans the property will know how to clean it to your standards.

A few things to note:
In between guests, take a quick walk-through of the whole property to check and make sure nothing is broken or missing. If it is broken, take pictures so you can deal with it later, after you've made the place ready for the next guests.

Every time you clean make sure you check on consumables such as soaps and shampoos, coffee and tea, and guest cleaning supplies. Refill where necessary and make a note of which supplies are running low and need to be repurchased.

Don't forget to wipe to high traffic surfaces such as door handles and light switches that can quickly get grimy. Also clean any windows that are smeared or dirty.

In the beginning, a turnaround may take longer than you think it will. My recommendation is to add extra time in between bookings so you will be able to finish on time. Once your cleaners learn a routine and start cleaning faster, you can reduce the time between bookings.

Deep Cleaning

Periodically, you will need to spend more time cleaning your Airbnb than can be done in a few hours turnaround. You should schedule a day for deep cleaning every three months or so. Book a day off on the listing calendar and prepare to get there early.

For this deep cleaning day, pretend you are spring cleaning your own home. Plan to complete at least the following tasks:

- Wash down all the walls

- Clean windows, inside and out

- Vacuum under furniture

- Clean behind and underneath the stove and refrigerator

- Shampoo upholstered furniture and rugs

- Change shower curtains

- Scrub grout

- Touch up any scuffs or chips in paint

- Wipe down baseboards and moldings

- Wipe down ceiling fans and light fixtures

To make sure you can get it done on time for the next booking, work with your cleaner or ensure the cleaning service you hired brings in enough team members to get it done in one day.

You may also find it necessary to book off a week once a year for some major refreshing of the property. Some rooms might be in need of a new paint job or wood floors could be ready for refinishing after heavy foot traffic. Schedule your contractors well ahead of time so these tasks get done within your timeframe.

Outdoor Maintenance

If your property is a condominium you shouldn't have to worry much about outdoor tasks. However, if there is a balcony, make sure it's as neat and tidy as you keep the inside.

A house involves a lot more ongoing maintenance tasks when it comes to landscaping, no matter what the season.

In the summer, the gardens and grass need to be watered and the lawn needs to be mowed. Plant low-maintenance perennials, such as hostas and shrubs because they are easy to maintain. Certain properties may need leaf removal in the fall and snow removal in winter. If you believe this will take too much of your time, it's probably best to contract a lawn maintenance company to take care of the landscaping tasks.

If you have a hot tub or pool, these will need ongoing attention to make sure the chemicals are balanced properly and the water is clean.

Guides for Guests

There are a few materials you want to include for your guests to inform them about your place and the surrounding areas. These include your guidebook, house manual and guestbook. In your Airbnb, set up a spot near the front door so your guests won't miss these books when they check in.

Guidebook
Creating a guidebook is a feature connected to your Airbnb profile. This guide can be confused with your house manual, but it is completely separate. The house manual is about the property and what is expected of

guests, while the guidebook is there to introduce them to the area they're visiting.

While the Guidebook can be accessible on Airbnb, you will want to have a hardcopy version of it at your property, too. Start with the online version to make your life easier. To create your guidebook, head on over to the main page of your Airbnb dashboard. Navigate to Menu > Guidebooks, and Airbnb will walk you through setting this up.

The purpose of the guidebook is to provide recommendations for the area in which your property is located. Include information about restaurants, theaters, parks, and tourist attractions.

Once you finish creating the online version, print out a copy to keep at your property. Make it presentable by adding the pages to a binder and keep it separate from your house manual.

Something I like to do to is go around to local restaurants and attractions to pick up copies of menus and brochures to include in the hardcopy binder. Local businesses are always happy to get free advertising. If I can manage to talk to the owner, I try to see if they can provide me with special discounts or coupons for my Airbnb guests.

If there are nearby hiking trails or walking tours of historic villages, another thing I do is print out maps or provide a QR code that links to the maps or more information.

Providing this information to your guests saves them the trouble of having to spend time searching for things to do online while they're on vacation. Touches like this assist in providing your guests the best experience, possible. It can also help your Airbnb stand out from those that only provide accommodation.

House Manual

Part of what makes an Airbnb property a success is a clear understanding of what is expected of your guests. This is where your house manual, comes in. Think of this as a user's manual for your property. Your house manual is a guide that clearly outlines essential information about the property.

Start with a short welcome page to highlight the most important items your guests will need to know. For example, Wi-Fi passwords and a number to contact in case of an emergency. You may provide a number that directs to you, your cleaner, a property management company, or a co-host.

Next, add the house rules of your property that were established in the last chapter. If you think of some more that you forgot, make sure to update your listing.

Finally, include any tasks guests need to complete before leaving. Keep in mind guest check-out tasks are a specific sub-set of rules that have created a fair amount of guest dissatisfaction recently. This is due to the fact that some hosts have started assigning guests a series of non-negotiable responsibilities that need to be completed before checking out. Apparently, one guest was told to mow the lawn – even after they paid a cleaning fee.

In these cases, guests may feel pressured into completing check-out tasks because they don't want bad reviews that will impact their chances of booking a future trip with Airbnb.

This is another time to think about your guest experience: put yourself in the guest's shoes and think about how they will feel once they arrive at your property. Your guest is booking your property because they are looking forward to a vacation free of the responsibilities of home. Is that the experience they will have?

Does your check-out list have simple tasks like taking the garbage out and running the dishwasher or is it full of major cleaning tasks like yard work or cleaning the toilets? If the guest sees a list of chores that need to be finished before checking out, that's not exactly the relaxing experience they were hoping for, is it?

You need to prioritize making your guests' lives easier when they book with you. Think of the tasks that are expected of you when you check out of a hotel. They only ask that you leave all towels on the bathroom floor and drop your key off at the front desk. That's it.

Airbnb itself isn't too thrilled about the uptick of guest tasks. In November 2022, Brian Chesky (if you remember is one of Airbnb's founders), clearly stated on Twitter:

"You shouldn't have to do unreasonable checkout tasks, such as stripping the beds, doing the laundry, or vacuuming. But we think it's reasonable to turn off the lights, throw food in the trash, and lock the doors—just as you would when leaving your own home."

Basically, if your check-out list looks and feels like "chores", consider the items you can remove.

Airbnb updated their process to be more transparent with guests about the rules and check-out procedures. Guests are now reminded of the rules hosts set as well as required check-out tasks. This keeps guests from any unpleasant surprises in terms of what's allowed or not once they arrive.

Four times before their arrival, they will be able to see your rules:

- In your listing.

- When guests confirm their booking.

- In the "Pack Your Bags" email.

- Finally, in the "Arrival Guide" shortly before their check-in.

Guestbook

The last book you should provide is a guestbook. Give your guests an opportunity to leave a note for you about their stay at your property. It's another way to make their visit to your Airbnb more special than going to a hotel.

Of course, you hope guests will leave a 5-star review online, but a guestbook is a way for them to make a more personal comment on their experience staying at your property.

The type of journal you choose for your guestbook is up to you – just don't choose an 8.5"x11" spiral bound notebook. You can go with a plain bound journal book with blank or lined sheets. Or be more creative and come up with a guestbook that reflects the theme of your property in some way.

Your guestbook will not only be appreciated by guests, but by you as well. If you're struggling to deal with a negative review, it can be a tangible reminder of how appreciative past guests have been.

Communication

From the moment a guest starts the booking process, you will have the opportunity to communicate directly with them. You will either receive a booking request or a message from them.

When a guest submits a booking request, know this is time sensitive and will expire after 24 hours, so don't wait long to respond. If you're not responding to a booking request within an hour of it being made, you are taking too long.

Look at it from the point of view of the guest. Whether they're planning a family vacation for three months from now, or a quick getaway in a couple of days, they will appreciate a quick response to confirm their booking. If you wait too long, they may simply move on to the next available property.

Also, if you fail to respond within the 24-hour window, you're impacting your host rating. Which, for Superhost status, you must maintain a 90% response rate. Obviously, you should get back to them as quickly as possible because this conversation may turn into a booking. Plus, too many non-responses can lead to your listing being blocked for a week.

Other times, guests will message you to find out more information about the property. In their message, they will indicate the dates they're considering, and they will more than likely ask you a question before making a booking request.

Don't be surprised if the questions are answered in your listing! No matter how detailed you wrote your listing, a lot of people don't take the time to carefully read through everything. Be prepared to answer questions that can be found in your listing and answer them with a friendly tone.

If the conversation does go well, you can "make the first move" to encourage them to book with you. On the right-hand side of the message, you will have the option to "pre-approve" a booking for them. The guest will receive this notification and will need to follow through and book on their end for the booking to happen.

Once you have a confirmed guest, you can now message the guest as much as you want. However, don't get too carried away because you don't want to risk annoying the guest. My recommendation is to message a guest no more than five times, total, from booking to post checkout. For example:

1. When you accept the booking, send a friendly note thanking them.

2. Message them a day or two before check-in to follow up with specifics like detailed directions and a picture of the front of the property.

3. On the day of their check-in, get back to them a few hours ahead of time with the front door code and any last-minute things they should know.

4. Depending on the length of their stay, message them a few days in to make sure things are going well and they have everything they need. Rule of thumb here is if they are staying for a couple of days, this isn't necessary. If they are staying a week or more, message them at least halfway through their stay.

5. Finally, on the day they check out, thank them for staying at your Airbnb and encourage them to leave you a review.

To avoid having to write the same responses over and over in each message, you can use quick replies to make your life easier. With quick replies, you can set up standard responses to be sent automatically and avoid having to type out repetitive messages to every guest.

To access quick replies, head over to the main page in your account and click on "Inbox". On the left, click the hamburger button (the three horizontal lines) to expand the menu.

Under Settings, select "quick replies" to set up your messaging for each type of reply. Airbnb provides a list of suggested topics, such as directions, house manual, house rules, and neighborhood.

Click on the reply you want to edit and fill in your response. If you want to personalize the message to your guest, this is where shortcodes come in. Shortcodes are commands that will automatically plug in guest-specific information into your message like their first name, booking dates, total trip price, or their home city.

Cancellations

The final, essential point I want to emphasize is once you have accepted a booking: **do not cancel**.

Yes, sometimes unavoidable emergencies arise and if you can prove that to Airbnb, you won't be penalized. For instance, if there's a serious issue like a gas leak or burst pipes on the property, you will not be charged cancellation fees. Reasons that are not acceptable include wanting the space for friends or family or discriminating against guests for any reason.

The penalties can be pretty serious. The maximum penalty for canceling less than 7 days before check-in is $1,000. Airbnb also blocks off those dates so the property cannot be re-booked and leaves an automatic review indicating the cancellation as a heads-up to future guests.

Finally, if you have canceled more than 1% of your bookings without an acceptable reason, you will not be able to obtain or maintain Superhost status. That's one cancellation per 100 bookings. In other words, cancel only if you absolutely have to.

Ratings and Reviews

Your reputation as a host depends on good ratings and reviews. Not only are they going to be your main selling point for future guests, good ratings will also move you further up the search results on Airbnb, eventually earning you Superhost status.

Obviously, you need to do everything you can to get rave reviews from your guests. Cleanliness, amenities, an accurate and truthful listing, easy check-in, and good communication are the most important aspects to pay attention to. These are also the things Airbnb lists as the essential elements of a guest experience that will lead to great reviews.

A great 5-star review is of course what we all want, every time. Once your guest leaves your property a review, pat yourself on the back and write a brief public response thanking them.

Negative reviews are harder to deal with. First, realize that sometimes people complain about minuscule things. A friend of mine received a less than 5-star review on a booking after her guest lifted the lid off the toilet tank and noted the liner was discolored. I'm pretty sure any future guest would see this review and shrug it off.

However, other complaints can definitely affect the desirability of your property. For instance, if I read a review complaining about hair on the shower floor, I would question their cleaning standards. Aside of making sure the hair isn't there in the first place, what would you say to respond to the review?

Here is how to *not* respond:
"We respect all guests and always give 5 stars to them. Even guests who messed the rooms and washrooms and blamed the hosts after leaving."

Looking at other reviews for this same Airbnb, I see lots of other complaints about cleanliness, so I know it's not an isolated incident.

On the other hand, this host does not appear to have learned from the negative reviews, either in her responses or by cleaning more thoroughly. The same complaints persisted even two or three years after the complaints started. After looking at these reviews, I'm definitely not going to be staying there if I'm a guest looking for a clean place to stay!

Don't be her. If you get feedback that there is an issue with your Airbnb, respond politely by thanking them for their input, apologizing for the problem, and promising things will be better in the future. Keep it brief and professional. Then move on.

Don't dwell on the poor rating. This is a "teachable moment" so learn from it and make sure it won't happen again in the future.

Unfortunately, not all reviews are fair and Airbnb is making it easier to request that a retaliatory review be removed. The example they give is a guest who breaks the no smoking rule on your property and leaves a negative review after being given a reimbursement request for deep cleaning. The process for disputing that review will be more streamlined in the future.

You will also have a chance to review your guests. It's a good practice to leave a review once your guests have checked out and you or your cleaners have been in to see how things look. Details are not too important here. Stick to the essentials another host would want to know when they receive a booking request: cleanliness, friendliness, and communication are key points to mention. Don't write a novel but a brief description of how the stay went.

Of course, if things did not go as smoothly with a particular guest, writing a review will be more challenging. It's important to make specific complaints rather than saying they were not good guests. Did they leave a mess behind? Were there noise complaints from neighbors? If you don't have those specifics to cite, don't leave a bad review. If you do have to write a bad review, give yourself 24 hours to calm down before posting it to make sure you're not overreacting.

Action Items to DO NOW!:

1. Test Drive Your Airbnb with a Soft Launch
Stay at your Airbnb a few nights yourself to make sure all your bases are covered. Then, invite a friend to stay as a guest at your Airbnb so they can provide feedback and let you know if there's anything you missed in your set-up.

2. Set Up Your Owner's Closet and Create a Cleaning Checklist
Stock your owner's closet with all your housekeeping essentials. Then, you and your cleaner (if you hired one) can establish a Cleaning Checklist and a regular turn-around cleaning routine.

3. Create Your Guidebook, House Manual, and Guestbook
Create a guidebook to be shown both in your listing and in hardcopy at the property. Then, create a house manual that includes your house rules and a guestbook for guests to document their experiences.

4. Establish Your Communication Procedure
Establish how many times and when to communicate with your booked guests, from the day they book to right after check-out. Set up your quick replies for repetitive messages.

5. Respond to Guest Reviews

Whether you get a positive or negative review, make it a rule to respond promptly, appropriately, and professionally.

CHAPTER SEVEN

Growing Your Business

After a few months of operating your Airbnb, you will start to get the hang of how things operate and work for your property. If your long-term goal is to turn hosting into a full-time job, now is the time to turn your focus to maximizing your process and the income you receive from your STR. Here are some ways to move towards that reality.

Listing on Other Sites

Know you are not limited to marketing your STR through Airbnb, only. Using their site doesn't mean you have an exclusive contract with them. Airbnb is only one of the platforms available for you to advertise your property and secure bookings.

Sites like Vrbo, Booking.com and FlipKey are vacation rental platforms similar to Airbnb and also places where you can list your STR property to expand its reach.

Vrbo has been around since 1995 and gets 16 million visitors a month. It's only for entire home rentals, so you know you're going to be advertising to your target market here. If you didn't already know, Vrbo is owned by Travel Away, which in turn is owned by Expedia. This means you can get exposure to the more than 700 million visitors to these sites every month, too.

Booking.com is another platform you can list your STR. This site allows users to search for and book a wide range of accommodations. In addition to traditional hotels, the platform also lists private accommodations such as vacation rentals and bed and breakfasts. This means that travelers who are searching for traditional hotel accommodations may come across listings for STRs on the platform as well and may choose to book a vacation rental instead of a hotel room. This can be beneficial for hosts as they may have a larger pool of potential guests through Booking.com.

FlipKey, a subsidiary of TripAdvisor, is another well-established vacation rental platform and allows hosts to leverage the vast audience of TripAdvisor to boost the visibility of their listings. With millions of monthly visitors, TripAdvisor's audience is one of the largest in the travel industry, and by listing their properties on FlipKey, short-term rental hosts can reach a wide audience of potential renters and increase their chances of bookings.

Another way to expand the reach of your STR is to set up a website for your property and manage your bookings there, instead. This will help you establish your brand identity independent of booking sites and you get to deal directly with guests without paying fees to a middleman.

If you are comfortable setting up a website on your own, Lodgify is a vacation rental software and website builder that allows you to create professional-looking websites you manage, yourself. The software offers a range of features including customizable templates, integration with booking channels, like Airbnb and Booking.com, and tools for managing rates, availability, and reservations.

Or, if this seems too overwhelming for you, you can always hire a professional website designer. When you choose this route, your goal should be to end up with an easy to use website that will have the same effect as listing on Airbnb. Therefore, working with someone who really knows their stuff and can understand your business goals will be a valuable asset as your business grows.

Finally, if you end up listing on multiple platforms, take caution to avoid double bookings! Channel managers can be set up to manage your bookings to avoid this. Using sites like Lodgify or Hostfully will remove availability on your calendars, across multiple platforms, once your property is booked.

Marketing

Utilizing social media to advertise your property is an effective method to attract more guests. Posting on these platforms is free, but you may choose to pay for advertising in order to reach a larger audience.

Instagram

Instagram is a great site to use to promote your Airbnb. If you search "#airbnb", you will see lots of properties from around the world featured in your feed.

If you already have a personal Instagram account, I recommend you create a separate business account specifically for promoting your Airbnb properties. This allows you to establish a distinct brand for your properties and ensures it is not mixed with your personal content. Since you only have one property at the moment, the name of this account should be the name of your property (you did give it a name, right?). Doing this immediately creates brand identification and is in itself an effective marketing tool.

Use a photo for your avatar that will be unique and convey a sense of what your place is like. Consider using the Hero photo from your listing so it is recognizable to viewers when they see it on Airbnb.

For your Instagram bio you have a limit of 150 characters, so take some time to craft an effective message without wasting any words. Remember the attention-grabbing statement you used in the first sentence of your property description when creating your listing? If it is not too long, add it to your bio. Just make sure you have characters left for some more details.

Next, include the location of your Airbnb - what city is it in? And what neighborhood? If it's a rural property, give a general sense of its proximity to nearby towns.

Finally, add a link to your Airbnb listing. Keep in mind, while you can add your listing link to Instagram, you can't add your Instagram link to your Airbnb profile or listing.

With your posts, you have two options: photos or videos. I suggest you use a mix of both to showcase your property and give viewers a taste of the experience they would have staying at your place.

To start, you can post all the photos from your photo shoot that appear in your listing. If you need more content, don't be afraid to post the photos that didn't make it to your listing page.

Don't post all your photos at once. The key here is to post them throughout the year – in two-to-three-times a week increments – consistently, on a regular basis. This will help you gain followers and build their interest in your property. If this starts taking up too much of your time, use an auto-scheduling platform like Hootsuite.

Get creative with your photos! You can really play up the change of seasons by showing the best of your property throughout the year. Another thing you can do is feature local events like festivals or parades that are coming up. Even a shot of a beautiful sunset from the patio can help establish the right mood.

Every time you visit your property, make it a point to take pictures you can post. If you have not been to your property in a while, a good idea I learned from my host friends is to post screenshots of your 5-star reviews from recent guests.

You also want to mix up the content and post a video once in a while. A good idea for video content is to do a virtual tour of your property. Then, once it is posted on Instagram, you can "pin" it to the top of your page so it can always be viewed. Then, for daily posts, you can include shorter videos of each room in your home, backyard features, or "live" videos of events in the area.

The great thing about Instagram is its editing features. With videos, for instance, you can use either voice-over narration or captions to add important information. There is also a music library with thousands of songs you can add to create an appropriate atmosphere.

It takes more than posting a good photo or video, though. You need to write a clear and exciting caption that describes the photo or video. You could even tell a story about what the photo represents. A long, well-written caption can draw the interest of potential guests and encourage them to click on your listing link.

Finally, using relevant hashtags is absolutely crucial to increase visibility of your property. Think of hashtags as keywords people use to search for your property and keep in mind, Instagram allows you to use up to 30 each post.

Right off the bat, you know you need to make it easy for people traveling to your area to find you. Start with #yourcity and #yourstate or #specificneighborhood, if it's relevant. If there's a notable attraction nearby, like a popular museum or a national park, add those as hashtags as well.

For more ideas, you will need to do some research to find relevant hashtags that will help more users find your property. One of the best ways to research is to look at the profiles of other hosts and take note of their hashtags and how they are using them. Then, take that data and create your own hashtags with your own style.

For maximum visibility, it's best to avoid using hashtags that have been overused as they will not be as effective. You can see the number of times a certain hashtag has been posted when you are typing in the caption area. When you start to type a hashtag, a list of hashtag suggestions and the number of public posts pops up. It is best to keep a list of more than 30 hashtags to use and use the 30 hashtags that coincide with the photo or video you are posting.

While an Instagram account is all I believe you need, Facebook, Pinterest and Tiktok are other great places to promote your property. Don't sign up for every platform. Think of your target audience and which one they use the most. That way you are not wasting your time trying to keep up with the many social media platforms out there.

Facebook
Facebook can be used to advertise your property and help you drive traffic to your listing like Instagram can. You don't even need a new account. Through your personal

account, you can create a separate page for your Airbnb property.

The setup is straightforward – you will need a cover image that is 1640 x 924 pixels for the top of your page. Then, proceed to set up the information about your property and post the same way you would on Instagram. While you can create text only posts, it's always good to include a photo or video to make the post stand out.

When your page is set up, invite friends and family to your page to start following you. Then, start asking guests. You can easily do this by adding a section in the hard copy of your house manual with a QR code that takes guests directly to your page.

Pinterest

For over a decade now, Pinterest has been a go-to site for a lot of people. In fact, over 400 million users perform 2 billion searches every month, making it a potentially powerful marketing tool if you know how to use it.

Airbnb's Pinterest account has boards covering topics like "Tiny Homes", "Amazing Views", and "Design". They have also created mini-itineraries called "Go Near Guides" to show travelers what they can visit near major cities.

If you already have a personal Pinterest account, create a business account. Pinterest offers free accounts (whether personal or business) and you have an opportunity to purchase ads if you want to increase your reach.

Start your page by adding your property or business name and a description. Next, create "boards" related to your property. For example, set up a board of local attractions or some of the scenic views nearby, and another board for nearby restaurants. Create as many as you would like while keeping in mind the activities and attractions around your property that will appeal to potential guests. This will enhance the likelihood of your board being discovered.

Then, the images you upload are called "pins" and can be "pinned", or assigned, to the appropriate "board". When creating a pin, upload a photo, add a title that describes the photo, and add a description.

You have 500 characters to use up in your description. Make the first 50 "attention grabbing" as those are the characters the user will see when they click on your pin. Finally, you can "Add a destination link". This link should be the link to take them to your listing to book a stay at your property.

TikTok
TikTok is another platform you can use to help bring in more bookings. Given the nature of the app, quirky

properties like hobbit houses or treehouses are more likely to get lots of views.

This platform allows you to create videos 15-seconds up to 10 minutes long. Like Instagram, there are a bunch of editing features to help you fine-tune your video before you post it.

Your goal is to create a following so your videos can rack up views. Aside of gaining organic followers from simply posting an engaging video, you can also interact with other users. For example, leaving comments on other videos can help you get noticed and attract more of your own followers.

Hashtags also play an important role on this site to help users search for and join existing conversations and communities that are already engaged with that topic. For example, a vacation rental in a specific location.

Including relevant hashtags with your videos improves the possibility of them being found by users searching for related topics. This means that if you use the right hashtags, you can tap into a wider audience that is looking for exactly what you have to offer.

Whichever social media sites you choose to use, take advantage of the free advertising you receive by creating your page and regularly posting to your growing audience.

If you're wondering about paid ads, I suggest waiting to take out ads on these sites once you see how much traffic is driven to your page without them. After all, if you are getting steady bookings without them, why spend the money?

Scaling Your Business

There are many strategies you can implement to help keep your business running smoothly. Building a team and automating as much of the operation as possible will maximize your time, profits and allow you to scale your business.

Automating

Once you have a good handle operating your one Airbnb property or want to move up to a multi-property business, start automating some day-to-day operations. This will help you free up your time, allowing you to focus on your larger goals.

Luckily, there are platforms out there that meet the needs of STR hosts who want to make their business more efficient. Sites like Guesty, Hospitable, or iGMS can help.

Whether your property is solely listed on Airbnb, or on multiple platforms, these sites will help you bring it all together to organize your bookings in one place.

For one, they provide automated messaging tools to help you message guests regardless of which site they used to reserve their stay. With their automated messages, you will be able to respond from an initial request to a thank-you after check-out.

A site like Guesty will help you manage your team by alerting your cleaning crew about check-out dates and how many guests will be arriving next. This is also one of the platforms that connect with Smart Keypads for your front door. Smart Keypads, like the Schlage Encode, sync up with Guesty and Guesty will change the codes for you with each new guest.

When using smart keypads, it is important to have a backup plan in case of WiFi outages. One effective solution is to purchase a key lockbox that can be mounted on an exterior wall of your property, making it easily accessible for both you and your guests in emergency situations.

As you can see, there are platforms available to help take a lot of the routine tasks of managing your property off your hands. Once you start using the ones that work for your business, you will have more free time to focus on scaling.

Team Building
While you may be able to operate a single Airbnb on your own, once you start to expand your operation you must

have people you can trust to maintain your high standards. Build a team you can rely on. The experience and insights you gained from doing the work yourself at first will help you build a strong team.

Cleaners are the ones who will be going in and out of your property on a regular basis. With that said, this means they will be the core of your Airbnb team as they are responsible for maintaining the property and ensuring that it is in a clean and presentable state for guests.

Cleanliness is the single most essential element of a successful STR business as you can see in reviews. Obviously, your cleaners will handle making sure everything is clean according to your standards. However, cleaners are also responsible for reporting any damages or missing items to you in a timely manner, so you can follow up with guests or Airbnb. Therefore, choosing a reliable and efficient cleaning crew is essential for the operation of your Airbnb business.

We've already discussed how to choose a cleaning crew in Chapter 4, but it cannot be emphasized enough that they are key to the operation of your Airbnb business. Consider offering bonuses every time you get a 5-star review for cleanliness.

If you are ever not satisfied with the cleaning crew's performance, be prepared to find a new cleaner as soon as possible. This will help you avoid negative reviews, losing your Superhost status or having your listing removed from the platform.

Cleaners are not the only team members you need. You will have other maintenance tasks to delegate.

We talked about how you should hire a landscaping company to mow the lawns in summer and clear away the snow in the winter. You should also have a general handyman on call to deal with issues like cleaning out gutters or touching up paint. If you're in an area where pests like termites or rodents are a problem, you will also need a pest control contractor.

Then, there are emergencies like a plumbing issue, broken appliance, or having a furnace or air conditioner break down. Rather than wait for the crisis, line up trusted local professionals ahead of time. You don't want an emergency to happen before you find someone. Plus, you will want someone to perform regular maintenance to prevent emergencies from happening as much as you can.

Finally, if day-to-day tasks start to become overwhelming, remember you have the option of contracting with an individual co-host or a professional property management service.

Delegating these tasks is crucial to scaling up your business. The time you save dealing with the day-to-day tasks yourself is time you can use to further expand.

Expanding

Once you start to receive a regular income stream from your first Airbnb property, you will most likely want to repeat your success by acquiring a second property.

You're probably wondering, *"at what point should I purchase the next one?"*.

When it comes to purchasing your next property, I suggest waiting until you have saved up enough money to cover six months' worth of expenses for your first property. This will provide you with a buffer, allowing you to cover the expenses of the first property while getting the second one established and generating income. This way you can make sure you have enough cash flow to handle both properties without putting yourself in a financial burden.

It's a good idea to make a second purchase in the same general vicinity as your first property. Not only do you already have a good feel for the local market, you already know how to work with any STR regulations in the area.

Most importantly, you can take advantage of using the same teams for cleaning and maintaining both properties.

Action Items to DO NOW!:

1. Develop Your Marketing Strategy
Choose which social media platform(s) you want to use.
Choose from Instagram, Pinterest, Facebook and TikTok
to expand visibility for your property. Start with free
accounts and buy ads to extend your reach if necessary.

2. Scale Up Your Operations
Once you get the hang of things, find out which property
management platform(s) will work best for you. You may
need to choose a couple of different ones, just make sure
they work with each other and save you time.

3. Build Your Team
Find professionals you can depend on to operate your
business while you work on ways to expand it.

CHAPTER EIGHT

Final Words

A cross the world, hosts have utilized similar strategies, like the ones you found in this book, to turn properties into income streams that have given them more independence. Now, you have the tools to help you become successful, too.

Together, we started with your initial decision to pursue the opportunity of creating an Airbnb business and developed a solid plan with long-term goals. From there, we discussed purchasing your first property, setting it up, and operating your business confidently and professionally.

This is not only the start of your new Airbnb business, it's the start of a new and exciting phase of your life. Whether you want to start a side-hustle for some extra monthly income or dream of expanding to a multi-property business as your full-time career, you now know what you need to be successful.

My hope is this book has given you the map you need to set out on the path to become an Airbnb Superhost, yourself. This is a rewarding journey that starts with a single step and leads to financial success when you put in the effort and commit to sticking with it.

Remember to keep the big picture of your 5-year plan in the back of your mind and continue to work towards it by accomplishing the goals you've set along the way. Don't be afraid to look back at your goals to remind yourself of what you are trying to accomplish. Sometimes re-reading your "why" will put things in perspective for you and will reignite your drive to achieve your goals.

Don't forget everyone runs into roadblocks from time to time. Whether it's a bad review or an uncooperative guest, don't allow temporary setbacks to bog you down. Reach out to other hosts who can give you encouragement or turn to your good reviews and guestbook entries to remind yourself of the positive experiences you do provide to guests.

Keep a positive mindset and you will be able to jump over and through all the hurdles. You will find it so much easier to weather the rough patches with a good attitude. This positivity will even communicate itself to your guests leading to even more success.

Now you have all the tools, go out there and use them. Your short-term rental business isn't going to start itself – believe in yourself. BET on yourself and know YOU CAN DO THIS!

Action Items to DO NOW!:

1. Put your best foot forward and step onto the path to success.
START and START *NOW*! DON'T procrastinate and know you are ready. If you need more help getting started, check out the Host Resources link on the next page.

2. If you enjoyed this book, ***please leave a review on Amazon*** to help others find the information they need to start their own Airbnb journey, too.

A Special Gift to My Readers

Access FREE Tools To Help You Become a Successful Host

I appreciate you taking the time to read my book! To show my gratitude, I have made additional downloadable resources to support you on your way.

Including:
Startup Costs Infosheet
Budget Worksheet
Competitor Research Worksheet
and more!

To Access:
Visit **www.davisjmiller.com/accesshostresources** OR
Scan the QR code below with your phone:

References

Adler, J. (2022, December 8). How to Start an Airbnb Business Successfully in 8 Clear Steps. *NorthOne Blog.* https://www.northone.com/blog/start-a-business/how-to-start-an-airbnb-business

Airbnb's New Feature Will Address Hidden Fee Complaints. (n.d.). https://www.apartmenttherapy.com/airbnbs-new-feature-hidden-fees-37184345

Airbnb Plus program standards - Airbnb Help Center. (n.d.). Airbnb. https://www.airbnb.com/help/article/2675

AirCover: An unmatched level of protection. (n.d.). Airbnb. https://www.airbnb.com/aircover

Araj, V. (2022, November 23). *What Is House Hacking And Is It Something You Should Be Doing?*

https://www.rocketmortgage.com/learn/house-hacking

Average Airbnb Occupancy Rates By City [2022] | AllTheRooms. (n.d.). https://www.alltherooms.com/analytics/average-airbnb-occupancy-rates-by-city/

Community Center. (2023, January 22). Airbnb Community. https://community.withairbnb.com/t5/Community-Center/ct-p/community-center

Deane, S. (2022, November 7). *2022 Airbnb Statistics: Usage, Demographics, and Revenue Growth*. Stratos Jet Charters, Inc. https://www.stratosjets.com/blog/airbnb-statistics/

Goldschein, E., & Orem, T. (2022, March 21). How to Start an Airbnb Business in 6 Steps — and Make Money. *NerdWallet*. https://www.nerdwallet.com/article/small-business/how-to-become-an-airbnb-host

Hostaway. (2022, December 21). *Is It Too Late to Start an Airbnb?* TurnoverBnB. Retrieved September 27, 2022, from https://turnoverbnb.com/is-it-too-late-to-start-an-airbnb/

Houst. (2019, April 23). How to Choose the Perfect Airbnb Investment Property for You. *Www.Houst.Com*. Retrieved September 27, 2022, from https://www.houst.com/blog/host-guides-how-to-choose-the-perfect-airbnb-investment-property-for-you

How to Start a Profitable Airbnb Business. (2022, October 14). *The Balance*. https://www.thebalancemoney.com/how-to-start-a-profitable-airbnb-business-4154273

iGMS Inc. (2022a, January 14). The Best Cities for an Airbnb Business in the US and Europe. *IGMS*. https://www.igms.com/best-cities-for-airbnb/

iGMS Inc. (2022b, July 18). *5 Shortcuts to Manage an Airbnb Remotely Like a Pro*. iGMS. https://www.igms.com/manage-airbnb-remotely/

iGMS Inc. (2023, January 13). Airbnb vs. Renting: Which Strategy Generates the Best ROI? *IGMS*. https://www.igms.com/airbnb-vs-renting/

Mburugu, C. (2020, November 1). *House Hacking: Your Guide to Living for Free in 2021*. Investment Property

Tips | Mashvisor Real Estate Blog.
https://www.mashvisor.com/blog/house-hacking-living-free-2021/

Mike Vestil. (2020, December 15). *How To Make Money on Airbnb Without Owning or Renting an Apartment* [Video]. YouTube. https://www.youtube.com/watch?v=86hr802Dpeg

Money Growth Project. (2021, May 15). *What Are The Biggest Problems Being An Airbnb Business Owner?* [Video]. YouTube. https://www.youtube.com/watch?v=LiaoM_jOqFg

Monteil, A. (2022, November 12). *Airbnb's New Feature Will Address Hidden Fee Complaints.* Apartment Therapy. Retrieved November 13, 2022, from https://www.apartmenttherapy.com/airbnbs-new-feature-hidden-fees-37184345

Pengue, M. (2022, June 12). Airbnb Statistics 2022: Demographics, Superhosts, Airbnb Plus | WBL. *Writer's Block Live.* https://writersblocklive.com/blog/airbnb-statistics/

Pros and Cons of Airbnb as an Investment Strategy. (2022, January 6). The Balance.

https://www.thebalancemoney.com/pros-and-cons-of-air
bnb-as-an-investment-strategy-4776231

Rakidzich, S. (2022, July 23). *From 1 airbnb to 25
airbnbs. Tips for building your team.* [Video]. YouTube.
https://www.youtube.com/shorts/KUwKpF8sRbg

Robuilt. (2021a, April 23). *How to
analyze a Short-Term Rental investment
property (Deal Analysis)* [Video]. YouTube.
https://www.youtube.com/watch?v=2MkZ66qTKs8

Robuilt. (2021b, July 5). *How to make an airbnb listing
LIKE A PRO (step-by-step tutorial)* [Video]. YouTube.
https://www.youtube.com/watch?v=pXK1NoWzx50

Robuilt. (2021c, August 16). *The 5 Airbnb
Business Models YOU NEED TO KNOW TO
GET STARTED TODAY* [Video]. YouTube.
https://www.youtube.com/watch?v=5lXrw7U3l7I

Robuilt. (2021d, August 23). *Literally EVERYTHING
you need to know to start an Airbnb
business (and manage remotely)* [Video]. YouTube.
https://www.youtube.com/watch?v=7UpFhAwAb8g

Robuilt. (2021e, December 27). *You'll lose thousands
hosting on Airbnb if you do this* [Video]. YouTube.
https://www.youtube.com/watch?v=7AgGw9TkLqM

Robuilt. (2022, March 31). *The downsides of managing an Airbnb* [Video]. YouTube. https://www.youtube.com/watch?v=YnHGdLCSAl8

Sean Rakidzich. (2019, September 11). *Airbnb Businesses Explained. Hosting, Cohosting and Rental Arbitrage business models* [Video]. YouTube. https://www.youtube.com/watch?v=QhLFouUYb8E

Sean Rakidzich. (2021a, April 22). *You Need This Airbnb Photos Reel Trick* [Video]. YouTube. https://www.youtube.com/watch?v=Pl_yz50KguI

Sean Rakidzich. (2021b, August 11). *Everything YOU need to Know to Start Your First Airbnb Property 2021* [Video]. YouTube. https://www.youtube.com/watch?v=ix05ZZvXnpg

Sean Rakidzich. (2022, January 28). *HOW TO START AN STR BUSINESS STEP BY STEP IN 2022* [Video]. YouTube. https://www.youtube.com/watch?v=RANqKCKK6QE

She's Off Script. (2021, January 28). *How To Run An Airbnb Business | No Money Down, Marketing, Cleaning* [Video]. YouTube. https://www.youtube.com/watch?v=RhWroH1_Ooo

STR University. (2017, October 19). *5 Overlooked Airbnb Listing Photos Most Hosts Forget (2017)* [Video]. YouTube. https://www.youtube.com/watch?v=ktl-f2jK6nU

Terms of Service - Airbnb Help Center. (n.d.). Airbnb. https://www.airbnb.com/help/article/2908

The difference between Airbnb Plus and Superhost - Airbnb Help Center. (n.d.). Airbnb. https://www.airbnb.com/help/article/2521

The Real Estate Robinsons. (2021, July 19). *Tips For Creating Your Airbnb House Rules* [Video]. YouTube. https://www.youtube.com/watch?v=gJUUGGix96s

Top Cities Where Airbnb Is Legal or Illegal. (2022, December 14). *Investopedia*. https://www.investopedia.com/articles/investing/08311 5/top-cities-where-airbnb-legal-or-illegal.asp

TurnoverBnB. (2022, April 1). *TurnoverBnB - Find vacation rental cleaners for your listings on Airbnb, Vrbo and schedule automatic cleanings*. https://turnoverbnb.com/?fbclid=IwAR3CW2B9ALIP ejNRlq-30jdVrkHQYhcvqc3dWZN2FZKMWFKMQ1 0-jyJBTbA

Made in the USA
Las Vegas, NV
05 November 2023